Microsoft O

explained

Books Available

By the same authors:

If you would like to purchase a Companion Disc for any of the listed books by the same authors, apart from the ones marked with an asterisk, containing the file/program listings which appear in them, then fill in the form at the back of the book and send it to Phil Oliver at the stipulated address.

Microsoft Office 2003 explained

by

N. Kantaris
and
P.R.M. Oliver

Bernard Babani (publishing) Ltd
The Grampians
Shepherds Bush Road
London W6 7NF
England
www.babanibooks.com

Please Note

Although every care has been taken with the production of this book to ensure that any projects, designs, modifications and/or programs, etc., contained herewith, operate in a correct and safe manner and also that any components specified are normally available in Great Britain, the Publishers and Author(s) do not accept responsibility in any way for the failure (including fault in design) of any project, design, modification or program to work correctly or to cause damage to any equipment that it may be connected to or used in conjunction with, or in respect of any other damage or injury that may be so caused, nor do the Publishers accept responsibility in any way for the failure to obtain specified components.

Notice is also given that if equipment that is still under warranty is modified in any way or used or connected with home-built equipment then that warranty may be void.

© 2004 BERNARD BABANI (publishing) LTD

First Published - March 2004

Reprinted - May 2005

British Library Cataloguing in Publication Data:

A catalogue record for this book is available from the British Library

ISBN 0 85934 544 0

Cover Design by Gregor Arthur
Printed and Bound in Great Britain by Cox & Wyman Ltd, Reading.

About this Package

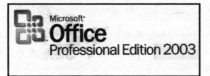

Microsoft Office 2003 explained has been written to help users to get to grips with the integrated components of this package, namely, the e-mail and desktop manager *Outlook* (redesigned and much improved in this version of Office), the word processor *Word*, the spreadsheet *Excel*, the presentation graphics *PowerPoint*, the application that helps you create and publish material *Microsoft Publisher* and the database *Access*. The latter is bundled with two of the six *Microsoft Office 2003* sets - the *Professional Edition* and the *Professional Enterprise Edition*, although it can be integrated with all other editions if bought separately. All these components were specifically designed for the *Windows 2000* (with Service Pack 3 or later) or Windows *XP* (recommended) environments.

Microsoft Office 2003 is an exciting new Office suite that will help with the new demands, challenges and opportunities to individuals and business. It offers new tools that use Web technology to provide enhanced single user or workgroup productivity and the ability to access and analyse important business data more efficiently with the adoption of the Extensible Markup Language (XML). This XML integration extends throughout the core of Office Professional Editions.

The individual applications which make up *Microsoft Office 2003* are designed to work together and have the same look and feel, which makes it easy to learn. For example, the majority of menus, toolbar buttons, and dialogue boxes are the same in each application, which gives them a consistent user interface.

The package incorporates several new features, as well as improvements on previous Office capabilities. These improvements (by application) include:

Microsoft Outlook 2003

Outlook has the biggest update of the Office applications. It now incorporates a Navigation Pane at the left of the screen which has entries for E-mail, Calendar, Contacts, Tasks, etc.

There is a New Mail Alert which displays at the bottom right corner of the screen to let you know that new mail has arrived while you are working with other applications. If you ignore it, it fades away. This message alert does not display when a PowerPoint slide show is running.

Outlook 2003 has a new Search Folders facility which allows you to use 13 folders as virtual stores for e-mail, such as unread mail, mail with attachments, mail to be followed up and even junk mail with new and powerful junk mail filters. By default, Outlook does not allow links to pictures on Websites which are used by spammers to verify that an e-mail address is alive and in use.

For those who are connected to a network, Outlook provides a new facility for viewing multiple users, Calendars side by side.

Microsoft Word 2003

Word has a new Reading Layout View which makes reading documents much easier. One of the buttons on the Reading Layout toolbar displays thumbnails of the pages of your document for easy navigation. However, a document displayed in Reading Layout View has nothing to do with how it will print out, which subtracts from its usefulness.

Word 2003 now has a new Research Task Pane (which also appears in some of the other Office applications), but which is particularly useful in Word as it combines the thesaurus and translation facility.

The Professional versions of Word support the Extensible Markup Language (XML).

Another new facility in Word is the **Check for Updates** option which, however, requires connection to the Internet, but ensures that the **Help** menu list remains up-to-date.

For those who collaborate in a large document production, Word provides a new Document Protection Task Pane which allows for a structured way of working. It allows the originator of the document to specify who can edit different parts of the document and impose formatting restrictions.

Microsoft Excel 2003

Excel is similar to Word in relying on multi-user files, so both packages share features related to collaboration between users and the use of the Extensible Markup Language (XML).

Excel also supports the new Research Task Pane which, just like in Word, contains the thesaurus and translation facility.

A new List functionality has been incorporated into Excel which allows users to select a range of data and quickly create a list. A new list is treated as a separate entity, therefore it supports the usual edits such as data selection or row inserts with a blue star indicating the insertion point as in Access.

Smart Tags can now be applied to individual cells. This can be extremely useful as you can link, for example, a person's name with entries in Outlook's Address Book, or a date to a personal calendar.

A number of improvements have been made to statistical analysis functionality, such as calculation of normal distributions, continuous probability distribution and sum of squared deviation functions

Excel 2003 supports 'ink markup' of spreadsheets using a pen input device on a Tablet PC. This allows you to add comments to a spreadsheet, such as annotating a workbook, before you send it to other users.

PowerPoint 2003

PowerPoint now includes the Research Pane with access to a thesaurus. A redesigned Slide Show toolbar offers better control during presentations, and users of a Tablet PC can add hand-written annotations to their slides. A new movie playing option allows a movie to play in full screen.

Smart Tags, first introduced in Windows XP, have now been incorporated into PowerPoint 2003 making it easier to adjust AutoCorrect options on the fly.

Perhaps the greatest improvement to PowerPoint is the ability to burn your presentation and its linked files to CD and use it on someone else's computer. The borrowed PC for your presentation, doesn't even have to have PowerPoint installed!

Publisher 2003

Microsoft Publisher looks and feels more like other Office 2003 applications. New features include paragraph formatting, bullets and numbering menu items, and the inclusion of a formatting toolbar similar to that found in Word.

Publisher 2003 now includes the ability to create e-mail newsletters, CD/DVD labels, enhanced greeting cards, and a lot more. These can be selected from the default New Publication Task Pane with the display of a range of additional thumbnails once an appropriate type of document has been selected.

Access 2003

Few improvements have been made in Access 2003 from previous versions of the program. The most notable ones are: the ability to change the default font and size for SQL queries, the new Dependencies Task Pane which allows you to quickly check the dependencies of an object so you don't delete it if it is being used by another object, and the new facility enabling you to back-up a currently open database without having to exit Access.

Like the other programs in the Office suite, Access can use the Windows SharePoint Services so, if you have access to it, you share data with other users.

* * *

The various applications within *Microsoft Office 2003* can either be used by themselves or made to share information. This book introduces each application by itself, with sufficient detail to get you working, then discusses how to share information between them. No prior knowledge of this package's applications is assumed. The book was written with the busy person in mind. It is not necessary to learn all there is to know about a subject, when reading a few selected pages can usually do the same thing quite adequately.

With the help of this book, it is hoped that you will be able to come to terms with Microsoft Office and get the most out of your computer in terms of efficiency, productivity and enjoyment, and that you will be able to do it in the shortest, most effective and informative way.

* * *

About the Authors

Noel Kantaris graduated in Electrical Engineering at Bristol University and after spending three years in the Electronics Industry in London, took up a Tutorship in Physics at the University of Queensland. Research interests in Ionospheric Physics, led to the degrees of M.E. in Electronics and Ph.D. in Physics. On return to the UK, he took up a Post-Doctoral Research Fellowship in Radio Physics at the University of Leicester, and then in 1973 a lecturing position in Engineering at the Camborne School of Mines, Cornwall, (part of Exeter University), where between 1978 and 1997 he was also the CSM IT Manager. At present he is IT Director of FFC Ltd.

Phil Oliver graduated in Mining Engineering at Camborne School of Mines in 1967 and since then has specialised in most aspects of surface mining technology, with a particular emphasis on computer related techniques. He has worked in Guyana, Canada, several Middle Eastern and Asian countries, South Africa and the United Kingdom, on such diverse projects as: the planning and management of bauxite, iron, gold and coal mines; rock excavation contracting in the UK; international mining equipment sales and international mine consulting. In 1988 he took up a lecturing position at Camborne School of Mines (part of Exeter University) in Surface Mining and Management. He retired from this in 1998, to spend more time writing, consulting and developing Web sites for clients.

Acknowledgements

We would like to thank friends and colleagues, for their helpful tips and suggestions which assisted us in the writing of this book.

Trademarks

Arial and **Times New Roman** are registered trademarks of The Monotype Corporation plc.

HP and LaserJet are registered trademarks of Hewlett Packard Corporation.

IBM is a registered trademark of International Business Machines, Inc.

Intel is a registered trademark of Intel Corporation.

Microsoft, **Windows**, and **Visual Basic**, are either registered trademarks or trademarks of Microsoft Corporation.

PostScript is a registered trademark of Adobe Systems Incorporated.

TrueType is a registered trademark of Apple Corporation.

All other brand and product names used in the book are recognised as trademarks, or registered trademarks, of their respective companies.

Contents

Appendix A

Appendix B

Glossary of Terms

Index

1

Package Overview

Microsoft Office 2003 is an integrated collection of powerful, full-featured, programs with the same look and feel that work together as if they were a single program. Office 2003 was specifically designed to allow you to work with your information data, either by yourself or to share such data with others, if you so wish, quickly and efficiently.

Microsoft Office 2003 comes in six flavours, each with a different mixture of applications (for an explanation on what these applications can do, see overleaf). The six sets are: Basic Edition, Student and Teacher Edition, Standard Edition, Small Business Edition, Professional Edition, and Professional Enterprise Edition. The various mixtures of applications for these six sets are as follows:

Office 2003 Unique Editions	Outlook 2003	Word 2003	Excel 2003	PowerPoint 2003	Publisher 2003	Outlook + B. C. M.*	Access 2003	InfoPath 2003
Basic Edition	☺	☺	☺					
Student and Teacher	☺	☺	☺	☺				
Standard	☺	☺	☺	☺				
Small Business	☺	☺	☺	☺	☺	☺		
Professional	☺	☺	☺	☺	☺	☺	☺	
Professional Enterprise	☺	☺	☺	☺	☺	☺	☺	☺

* In the table on the previous page, B.C.M. stands for Business Contact Manager.

Note: The Professional and the Professional Enterprise Editions also include support for the Extensible Markup Language (XML) and Information Rights Management (IRM) content creation and authoring. This last capability helps businesses to control who has access to sensitive information when colleagues work on a document together.

The Microsoft Office 2003 applications have the following main functions:

Outlook
An e-mail and Personal Information Manager (PIM) that provides a full set of multi-user, group-scheduling PIM functions. Three of the six versions now include a new Business Contact Manager add-on that connects small businesses to their customers through integrated e-mail marketing and to their business data through integration with other Office Suite applications. This is useful for recording notes and pictures against contact records.

Word
A Word processor that offers almost every imaginable feature, including background spelling and grammar checking, integrated drawing tools, WYSIWYG editing views, Smart Tags and Task Panes. The new version also includes enhanced merge and markup capabilities.

Excel
An electronic spreadsheet that allows the creation of 3D super-spreadsheets by using multi-page workbooks which support 3D *drill-through* formulae, and includes a long list of 'goal-seeking', 'what- if?' analysis tools and an excellent set of database capabilities.

PowerPoint	A presentation graphics application that allows the creation of slide shows for training, sales and other presentations, and includes, amongst other capabilities, object animation, speaker notes, and recorded voice-overs.
Publisher	An application that allows the design and creation of printed documents with the help of publication templates. It can auto-fit text to frame sizes, provide inter-frame text flow options, and auto-wrap text around irregular images.
Access	A database management system (DBMS) that includes a full set of WYSIWYG design tools for database, forms, queries and reports, plus a full Visual Basic derived programming language for developing specific applications.
InfoPath	A new application in the Office Professional Enterprise Suite that streamlines the process of gathering information by enabling teams and organisations to easily create and work with rich, dynamic forms.

Additional add-ins to the Office Editions, which can be purchased separately, are:

OneNote	A new application in the Office Suite that enables you to capture, organise, and reuse notes you gathered on your computer, be it a desktop, laptop, or a Tablet PC. It stores all your notes in one place and gives you the freedom to work with them later on.
Office Visio	A drawing and diagram making application that helps you to easily transform traditional data into diagrams.

FrontPage   An application that gives users tools to create and manage Web sites, whether personal or corporate Web pages on intranet or Internet sites.

All Office 2003 applications have a built-in consistency which makes them easier to use. For example, they all have standardised toolbars and consistent menus, commands, and dialogue boxes. Once you become familiar with one application, it is far easier to learn and use the others.

Just like its predecessors, Office 2003 applications make use of what is known as IntelliSense, which anticipates what you want to do and helps you to produce the correct result. Amongst other common code, first introduced in Office 95, then improved in Office 97 and Office XP, are the Wizards which can help you simplify everyday and/or complex tasks, and the support for Microsoft Visual Basic for Applications, which gives you a powerful and flexible development platform with which to create custom solutions.

Office 2003 supports Smart Tags and Task Panes, first introduced in Office XP. Smart Tags anticipate what you might want to do next and pop up a button near where you are working, offering relevant suggestions. For example, when copying then pasting text into a document causes a Paste Options Smart Tag to pop up giving you the opportunity to select a style. Other context sensitive Smart Tags allow you to access names, addresses and telephone numbers from your Outlook folder which can save you time and bother. These provide a welcome addition to Word's ability to recognise Web links and e-mail addresses.

Task Panes utilise the screen space available when writing portrait-orientated documents to provide an area in the right-hand side of your screen where information relevant to what you are doing at the time is given. For example, when you first start working within an application, you are offered options to open new documents or search for existing documents. As the type of work changes, the contents of the Task Pane change to reflect the type of work you are doing at the time.

Office 2003 supports the Document Recovery feature first introduced in Office XP. Gone are the days when unless you saved your work every second you lost everything when a program error occurred. Now Office 2003 gives you the opportunity to save your work immediately after a program error occurs.

Other features in Office 2003 include the ability to Send for Review documents which you have created. For example, if you are involved in a team project, you can allocate different review mark-up and changing privileges to your colleagues so that you can see the changes applied by everyone. You are then in a position to accept or reject these changes.

To take advantage of the SharePoint Services of Office 2003, you require connection to a Windows 2003 server. This enables colleagues to create task and contact lists, calendars and planners, discussion groups and easy accessibility to common documents.

Finally, Office 2003, just as Office XP, uses the usual activation system. To use Office 2003 more than 30 days, you must register it via the Internet or by telephone.

Hardware and Software Requirements

If Microsoft Office is already installed on your computer, you can safely skip this and the next section of this chapter.

The minimum requirements for Office 2003 are an IBM-compatible PC with Pentium 133 MHz processor, 64 MB of RAM and 245 MB of hard disc space. However, to install and use Microsoft Office Professional 2003, you need a Pentium 233 MHz or higher processor - Pentium III recommended, with 128 MB of RAM, and at least 400 MB of hard disc space. In addition, you need the following:

• Windows 2000 (with Service Pack 3 or later), or Windows XP or later (recommended) as the operating system. If you have an earlier version of Windows you must first upgrade to one of the above versions before you can install Office 2003.

- An additional 8 MB of RAM minimum for each Office application (Word, Excel, PowerPoint, Outlook, Access, FrontPage, Publisher, OneNote or InfoPath) when running simultaneously.

- An additional 290 MB required on the hard disc where the operating system (such as Windows XP) is installed for optional installation file cache.

- CD-ROM drive.

- Super VGA (800x600) or higher resolution video adapter with a minimum of 256 colours.

- Microsoft Mouse, IntelliMouse, or compatible pointing device.

- For sound and other multimedia effects, a multimedia compliant PC is required, including a Windows compatible sound card.

- To run Microsoft Office 2003 from a network, you must also have a network card.

To use the optional Business Contact Manager you need a Pentium III with 450 MHz or higher processor, 256 MB of RAM or above, and an additional 190 MB of hard disc space. These are also recommended if you choose to run Office 2003 with multimedia support, or intend to use reasonable sized application documents, and speech recognition.

Installing Microsoft Office 2003

Installing Office on your computer's hard disc is made very easy using the SETUP program, which even configures Office automatically to take advantage of the computer's hardware. One of SETUP's functions is to convert compressed Office files from the CD-ROM, prior to copying them onto your hard disc.

Note: If you are using a virus detection utility, disable it before running SETUP, as it might conflict with it.

To install Microsoft Office, place the distribution CD in your CD drive and close it. The auto-start program on the CD will start the SETUP program automatically. If that does not work, click the *start* button, and select the **Run** command which opens the Run dialogue box, as shown in Fig. 1.1.

Next, type in the **Command Line** box:

D:\setup

In our case we used the CD-ROM in the d: drive; yours could be different.

Fig. 1.1 The Run Dialogue Box.

Clicking the **OK** button, starts the installation of Microsoft Office 2003. SETUP first displays a screen informing you that the program is preparing the Office 2003 Installation Wizard, then displays the screen in Fig. 1.2.

Fig. 1.2 Product Key Screen.

We suggest that you follow the instructions displayed on the screen. Clicking the **Next** button, causes SETUP to go through the following procedure:

- Asks for your name and organisation.

- Asks you whether to Upgrade or choose another type of installation, as shown in Fig. 1.3. Your choice depends on the type of Office software purchased (upgrade being a lot cheaper than the other option). If you choose to upgrade, SETUP searches your system's discs for installed Office components. Either installation choice prompts you to supply the path to the directory where you want to install Office 2003, and then checks your system for available hard disc space.

Fig. 1.3 Choosing the Type of Office Applications to be Installed.

- Displays a summary of the Office 2003 applications to be installed which depend on the choice made by you in Fig. 1.3 above, assuming your choice is legal - you cannot choose a complete install with an Upgrade CD!

- Clicking the **Install** button starts copying files to your computer's hard disc and removes all previous versions of the software, then displays the screen in Fig. 1.4.

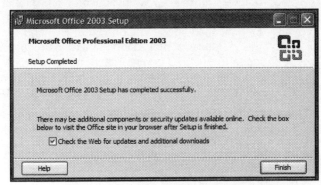

Fig. 1.4 The Completed Installation Screen.

To start one of the installed Office 2003 applications, use the *start*, **All Programs** command and select the **Microsoft Office** entry from the cascade menu, as shown in Fig. 1.5.

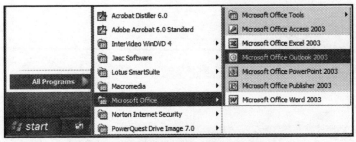

Fig. 1.5 The Microsoft Office Cascade Menu.

Clicking on one of the Office applications starts the Activation Wizard. Activation is not the same as registering the software which gives you access to the Microsoft Office product support and product update information. Activation allows you to run the software for no more than a given number of times, before major application features are switched off. During activation, the product ID and a non-unique hardware identification are sent to Microsoft, but it does not include personal information or any data held on your computer.

The product ID is generated from the product key used to install the software and a generic code representing the version and language of the Microsoft Office being activated. The non-unique hardware identification represents the configuration of your PC at the time of activation. The hardware identification identifies only the PC and is used solely for the purpose of activation. Office can detect and accept changes to your PC configuration. Minor upgrades will not require re-activation, however, if you completely overhaul your PC, you may be required to activate your product again.

The first Office 2003 Activation Wizard screen is shown in Fig. 1.6 below.

Fig. 1.6 The Office Activation Wizard Screen.

As you can see, in this Wizard screen you can choose the method of activation; via the Internet, or by telephone. If you choose to activate your product through the Internet and you are not already connected, the Wizard will help you get connected.

Adding or Removing Office Applications

To add or remove an Office application, left-click the *start* button and click the **Control Panel** option on the Windows

pop-up menu, as shown in Fig. 1.7. This opens the Control Panel dialogue box shown in Fig. 1.8.

Next, double-click the **Add/Remove Programs** icon, pointed to in Fig. 1.8 to open the Add or Remove Programs dialogue box shown in Figure 1.9 on the next page.

Fig. 1.7 The Windows Start Menu.

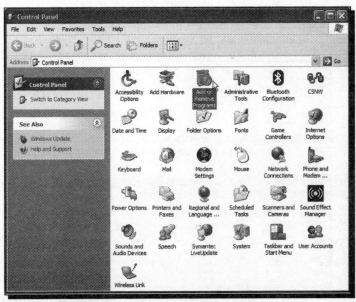

Fig. 1.8 The Control Panel Dialogue Box.

Next, locate the Microsoft Office program and click the **Change** button, as shown below.

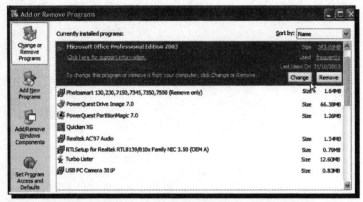

Fig. 1.9 The Add/Remove Programs Dialogue Box.

This causes SETUP to display the Maintenance Mode Options screen shown in Fig. 1.10:

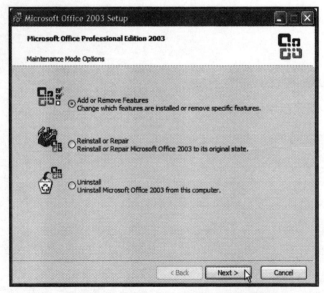

Fig. 1.10 The Office Maintenance Mode Options Screen.

Note the **Reinstall or Repair Office** button on the screen of Fig. 1.10. Use this to reinstall the whole of Microsoft Office, or to find and fix any errors in your original installation.

Selecting the **Add or Remove Features** option and pressing the **Next** button opens up the dialogue box of Fig. 1.11.

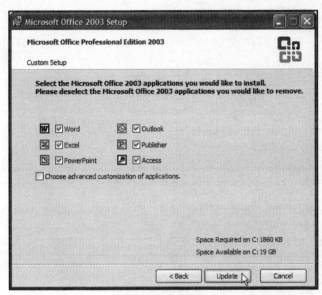

Fig. 1.11 The Custom Setup screen for Office Applications.

Note that on this screen you can either deselect an application to remove it or, if not installed, select it to install it. If you would like to change the way components of a certain application are installed (for example some components are only installed on first use and you might like to change this choice), select the **Choose advanced customization of applications** box which changes the **Update** button to **Next**. Clicking this button displays the Advanced Customization screen shown in Fig. 1.12 on the next page.

Fig. 1.12 The Advanced Customization Screen for Office Applications.

A plus (+) sign to the left of an application indicates sub-features which you can add or remove from the Office installation, or change how the feature is installed by clicking its symbol and then selecting another symbol from the list that appears, as shown in Fig. 1.13.

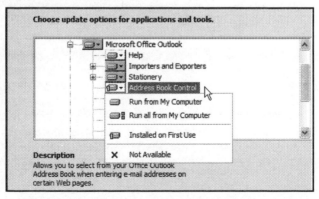

Fig. 1.13 The Update Options Screen for Office Applications.

The Mouse Pointers

In Microsoft Office applications, as with all other graphical based programs, using a mouse makes many operations both easier and more fun to carry out.

Office 2003 makes use of the mouse pointers available in Windows, some of the most common of which are illustrated below. When an Office application is initially started up the first you will see is the hourglass, which turns into an upward pointing hollow arrow once the individual application screen appears on your display. Other shapes depend on the type of work you are doing at the time.

The hourglass which displays when you are waiting while performing a function.

The arrow which appears when the pointer is placed over menus, scrolling bars, and buttons.

The I-beam which appears in normal text areas of the screen. For additional 'Click and Type' pointer shapes, specific to Office XP applications, see the table overleaf.

The 4-headed arrow which appears when you choose to move a table, a chart area, or a frame.

The double arrows which appear when over the border of a window, used to drag the side and alter the size of the window.

The Help hand which appears in the Help windows, and is used to access 'hypertext' type links.

Office 2003 applications, like other Windows packages, have additional mouse pointers which facilitate the execution of selected commands. Some of these are:

↓	The vertical pointer which appears when pointing over a column in a table or worksheet and used to select the column.
→	The horizontal pointer which appears when pointing at a row in a table or worksheet and used to select the row.
↗	The slanted arrow which appears when the pointer is placed in the selection bar area of text or a table.
↔‖↔	The vertical split arrow which appears when pointing over the area separating two columns and used to size a column.
≑	The horizontal split arrow which appears when pointing over the area separating two rows and used to size a row.
+	The cross which you drag to extend or fill a series.
✎	The draw pointer which appears when you are drawing freehand.

Word 2003 also has the following Click and Type pointer shapes which appear as you move the I-beam pointer into a specific formatting zone; their shape indicating which formatting will apply when you double-click.

I≣	Align left	≣I	Align right
I̲	Centre	I≣	Left indent
I▦	Left text wrap	▦I	Right text wrap

Fig. 1.14 The Click and Type Pointer Shapes in Word 2003.

If you don't see the Click and Type pointer shapes, check that the facility is turned on. You can do this by using the **Tools**, **Options** command, then click the Edit tab, select the **Enable click and type** check box, and press **OK**.

Getting Help in Office 2003

No matter how experienced you are, there will always be times when you need help to find out how to do something in the various Office applications. Office is after all a very large and powerful suite of programs with a multitude of features. As we shall see, there are several ways to get help now, including the Office Assistant, or Clippy as he is called by Microsoft, although by default it is switched off. It can be activated by using the **Help**, **Show the Office Assistant** menu command within any of the Office applications.

The Research Task Pane

Fig. 1.15 The Research
Task Pane.

To quickly access Help, you can use the **Type a question for help** box on the menu bar or the **Search for** box halfway down the Research Task Pane shown in Fig. 1.15, by typing a question and pressing the <Enter> key. However, both these help facilities rely on getting the answers from the Internet, and a connection is necessary. A list of help topics is then displayed.

To see more Task Pane topics, left-click the small triangle to the right of the **Getting Started** Task Pane (pointed to in Fig. 1.15). Selecting a different Task Pane from the displayed list and clicking on a topic, opens the Help system and provides you with an answer. Some topics require connection to the Internet, others do not. The Research Pane is particularly useful in Word, as it combines the thesaurus and translation facilities.

The Office Assistant

The Office Assistant is turned off by default in this version of Office. When activated, it first appears as we show on the left,

and automatically provides Help topics and tips on tasks you perform as you work. To find out how it works, start an Office application (we used Word) and use the **Help**, **Show the Office Assistant** menu command to open Clippy, shown here on the left.

Now left-click him and select to open the 'What would you like to do?' box, shown in Fig. 1.16. To get help you simply type your query here and click the **Search** button. The search results appear on the Research Task Pane.

Fig. 1.16 Using the Office Assistant.

If you like, you can customise the Assistant, and decide if you want it to automatically display tips, messages, and alerts, make sounds, move when it's in the way, and guess a Help topic that it thinks you may need.

You can also switch it off once you have mastered a particular Office application, or cannot cope with its intrusions any more! All of these features are controlled from the box shown in Fig. 1.17 which is opened by clicking the **Options** button shown in Fig. 1.16.

Fig. 1.17 The Left-click Assistant Menu

To change the shape of your Office Assistant (there are eight shapes to choose from), either left-click the Gallery tab of the dialogue box shown in Fig. 1.18, or right-click the Office Assistant and select the **Choose Assistant** option from the displayed menu, as shown in Fig. 1.17.

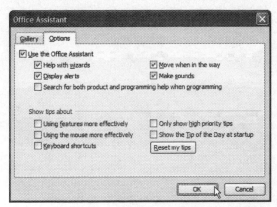

Fig. 1.18 The Office Assistant Options Box.

Either of these actions displays the following dialogue box (Fig. 1.19) in which you can select your preferred Assistant shape by left-clicking the **Next** button.

Fig. 1.19 The Office Assistant Gallery Box.

The eight shapes of the available Assistants are shown in Fig.1.20 on the next page. We find the Office Assistant's animated characters to be very clever and amusing, but must admit that like most people we prefer to work with the facility turned off. To do this, make sure the **Use the Office Assistant** option is not selected in the Options box shown in Fig. 1.18.

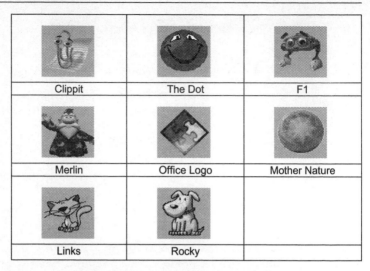

Clippit	The Dot	F1
Merlin	Office Logo	Mother Nature
Links	Rocky	

Fig. 1.20 The Available Office Assistant Shapes.

The Built-in Microsoft Help System

To illustrate the built-in Microsoft Help System we will use here the word processing application (Word 2003) - other Office applications operate in exactly the same way. If you turn the Office Assistant completely off (as described on the previous page) and press the **F1** function key, or click the **Help** toolbar button shown here, or use the **Help**, **Microsoft Office Word Help** menu command, Help will be accessed directly through the Help window. This is the way we prefer to work.

When first opened, the Microsoft Word Help will be displayed in the right-hand pane as shown in Fig. 1.21 on the next page. Clicking the **Table of Contents** link (pointed to in Fig. 1.21), opens up a list of available help topics in the form of closed books. Left-clicking one of these books displays a further list of topics (Fig. 1.22), also shown on the next page. This gives a quick way to get information on **What's new in Microsoft Office Word 2003**, **Getting Help**, **Using Microsoft Office**, etc. Each of these has a very colourful button you can press to display further information.

Fig. 1.21 Microsoft
Word Help.

Clicking any these 'hypertext links'
opens the relevant Help page in a
separate window, which might
contain further links. We suggest
you try looking up 'what is new' in
every Office application you use - it
is an excellent starting point in
learning how to use the Office Help
System. Other topics can always be
explored later.

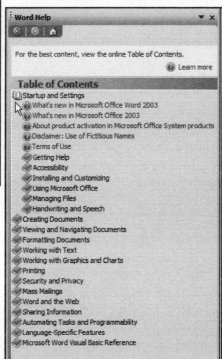

Fig. 1.22 Help Contents List.

The Web browser
type buttons at the
top of the help
screen in Fig. 1.22
(also shown below),
have the following
functions:

Click the first button
if more than one help screen has been opened to go back to
the previously opened help screen. Click the second button if
you have moved back to a previous help screen to move
forward through opened help screens. Click the third (Home)
button to jump to the Getting Started help screen (Fig. 1.15).

The Word Help system is very comprehensive but it is not always easy to find the information you are looking for. It usually pays to select the feature, or object, you want details on before accessing Help, you may then get exactly the right information straight off.

ScreenTips

If you want to know what a menu command or button does, or if you want to know more about an option in a dialogue box, you can also get ScreenTips help. These can be accessed in two ways:

- To see the name of a toolbar button, rest the pointer over the button and its name will appear.

- In a dialogue box, click the Help button ▓ in the top right corner of the box, and then click the option.

2

Microsoft Outlook 2003

Microsoft's Outlook 2003 is a powerful personal information manager (PIM) - a kind of Filofax - that supports a full set of multi-user, group scheduling PIM functions. Outlook can be made the centre of activity for all the other Office 2003 applications; it can be used *online* or *off-line*.

To work online, your computer must either be connected to a shared network resource, which is imperative if you are planning to use Outlook's group-scheduling features, or you must be connected to the Internet via a modem.

Starting Outlook 2003

Outlook 2003 is started in Windows by clicking on the **Microsoft Outlook** button, shown here, on the *start*, **All Programs**, **Microsoft Office** cascade menu (see Fig. 1.5).

When you start Outlook 2003 the program momentarily displays its opening screen (Fig. 2.1), and then displays the Personal Folders screen shown in Fig. 2.2 overleaf.

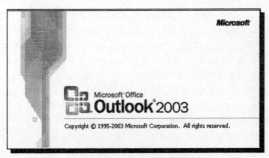

Fig. 2.1 Outlook's Opening Screen.

Fig. 2.2 The Outlook Personal Folders.

Microsoft has introduced a Navigation Pane at the left of Outlook's screen (Fig. 2.2 above), which has entries at the bottom-half of the pane for activities such as Mail, Calendar, Contacts, Tasks, as well as a few additional shortcuts. Clicking any one of these major Outlook activity buttons displays related folders on the upper part of the Navigation Pane.

Most of the Mail folders are self-explanatory, with Inbox being the folder containing all the received e-mails, Outbox being the folder containing the e-mails you have prepared off-line ready to be sent when you connect to the Internet, Draft is the folder in which you save the e-mails under preparation that you intend to complete later. Other folders are used for housekeeping, such as the Deleted Items folder used to find deleted items and reinstate them, the Sent Items folder which holds a copy of all items you have sent, the Junk E-mail folder which can be made to hold filtered junk e-mail, and the Search Folder for holding specified e-mail searches.

Parts of the Outlook Screen

Before we go any further, take a look at the contents of Outlook's **Inbox** screen which can be displayed

📄 Inbox

by clicking the **Inbox** button on the Navigation Pane, shown here and pointed to in Fig. 2.3 below. The screen contains three distinct areas, Navigation Pane, Message list, and Reading Pane.

Fig. 2.3 The Outlook Today Screen.

For an explanation of the various screen areas, please refer to Appendix A, and for the menu bar options to Appendix B.

Do read the message from Microsoft which is to be found in your **Inbox**. It gives basic information on the new features of the program, such as the new layout and the automatic grouping of messages, the new junk e-mail filter, Navigation and Reading Panes, use of Quick Flags for responding to messages, the use of Search Folders, and the display of Calendars.

To find out more about Outlook in general, and its new features in particular, left-click the Help button on the extreme right of the Toolbar, shown to the left, to display the Help Pane shown in Fig. 2.4 below.

Fig. 2.4 The Outlook Help Pane.

As you can see, this is similar to the Research Task Pane we discussed in Chapter 1, page 17 (see Fig. 1.15). To display information on any of the listed topics which display in blue (indicating hypertext links), simply move the mouse pointer onto one of these and when the pointer changes to a hand, click the left mouse button.

Clicking the link Table of Contents, pointed to in Fig. 2.4, displays a list of help topics in the form of closed books. Left-clicking each book displays additional topics under it, which when clicked in turn, display the required information in a separate window which opens up next to the Help Pane, as shown in Fig. 2.5 on the next page.

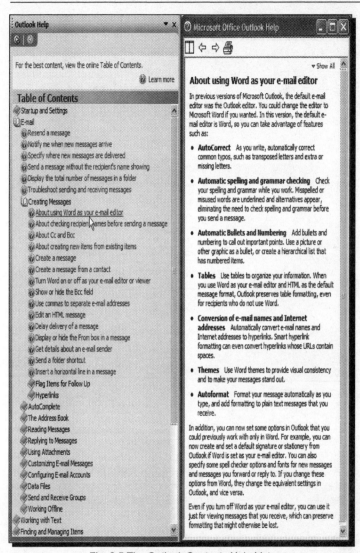

Fig. 2.5 The Outlook Contents Help List.

We suggest you use this Help facility to find more about a specific topic you might be working with if you need more information. Training is available on various topics (see appropriate link in Fig. 2.4), but only online.

Importing Data into Outlook

If you already hold personal or business information, such as contacts or tasks to perform, on another program, now is the time to import these into Outlook. To begin the process, use the **File, Import and Export** command which starts the Import and Export Wizard, the first screen of which is shown in Fig. 2.6.

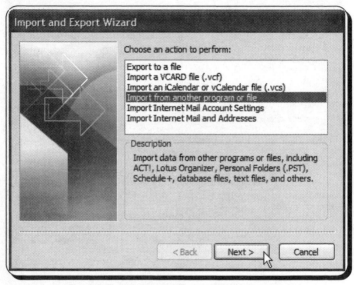

Fig. 2.6 The Import and Export Wizard Screen.

Next, highlight the 'Import from another program or file' entry and press **Next**, which causes the Wizard to display a list of possible organiser-type formats that it can handle by displaying the screen in Fig. 2.7.

We will attempt to import information from Lotus Organizer 5.0, our previously used scheduler. Selecting the type of file you want to convert and pressing the **Next** button displays the next Wizard screen in which you are asked to locate the file to be converted, as shown in Fig. 2.8. The program might ask you to load the necessary translator from the Office 2003 distribution CD if it is not already installed.

Fig. 2.7 Selecting a File Type to Import.

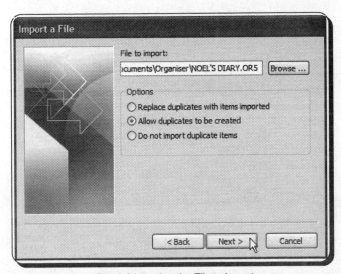

Fig. 2.8 Locating the File to Import.

In our case the Wizard found the required file and proposed to carry out six actions, as detailed below. In your case these will most certainly be different.

Fig. 2.9 Proposed Actions to be Taken During Data Conversion.

Pressing the **Finish** button, starts the conversion process, during which you are informed exactly what is going on.

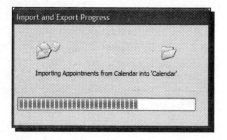

In our experience the data conversion was faultless. We were particularly impressed that the extensive information in our **Contacts** folder was converted fully and accurately. Obviously we cannot show you the complete outcome of this process, as it contains private and sensitive information, but you will see some conversion entries as we examine the individual sections of Outlook.

Using the Calendar

Before we start entering information in our Calendar, let us take a look at its opening screen.

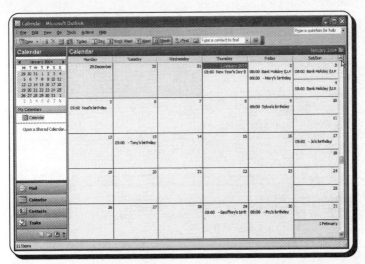

Fig. 2.10 The Opening Calendar Screen in Monthly View.

As you can see, certain information was transferred from our previous organiser and is shown here in Fig. 2.10. Changing the range of days you are viewing within a month could not be simpler; just click the scroll buttons of the vertical scroll bar - clicking the upper scroll button displays earlier dates, while clicking the lower scroll button displays later dates. The days in the current month are shown in white, while the days of earlier and later months are shown in grey.

To see the Calendar in daily or weekly view, simply click the appropriate button on the Calendar Toolbar, shown below.

Or use the **View** command, then select **Day**, **Work Week**, or **Week**.

Viewing Appointments

All the details of appointments, events or meetings can be viewed in Outlook whether you are in the Daily, Weekly, or Monthly view; you can see the date, time, and the description. You also have the facility to use colours and symbols to indicate whether the appointment is recurring, tentative, private, etc., and whether a reminder has been set, shown by a small bell. In Fig. 2.11 the Calendar is displayed in Daily View.

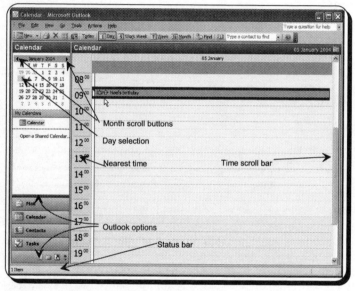

Fig. 2.11 The Calendar Display in Daily View.

To look at another day, left-click on the day you want to look at on the monthly calendar at the top left of the screen.

Information relevant to an appointment or meeting is also displayed in the Appointment dialogue box (to see one, double-click on a day on the Calendar - to be discussed next). To organise a meeting, however, you will need to click the Scheduling tab of the Appointment dialogue box.

Appointments, Meetings, and Events

Before you start scheduling an appointment, meeting or event, it is necessary to look at the following definitions:

- An appointment does not involve other colleagues or resources, and can be recurring, that is, it can be repeated on a regular basis.

- A meeting is an appointment that involves other people and possibly resources, and can also be recurring.

- An event is an activity that lasts one day, or more, such as attendance at an exhibition or conference. An annual event occurs yearly on a specific date. Events and annual events do not occupy blocks of time in your Calendar; instead, they appear as a banner below the current day heading.

Entering Appointments

We will now create a recurring appointment to, say, meet Section Managers, that takes place on Wednesday every four weeks starting at 10:00 a.m. on 7 January and lasts for 2 hours. To do so, click on 7 January on the calendar to the left of the entry area, move the cursor to 10:00 a.m., click the **New** button and select **Appointment** from the drop-down

menu shown here to the left. This opens the Appointment dialogue box displayed in Fig. 2.12 on the next page in which you can type 'Managers' meeting' in the **Subject** box, and 'My Office' in the **Location** box, set the **End** time to 12.00, click the **Reminder** box and select 15 minutes, and then press the **Recurrence** button on the Toolbar.

In the Appointment Recurrence dialogue box (Fig. 2.13), click the **Weekly** radio button and in the **Recur every** box, pointed to, type '4', fill in the rest of the information as shown, and click **OK**. Finally, click the **Save and Close** button located at the top of the first dialogue box.

Fig. 2.12 Entering Information in the Appointment Dialogue Box.

Fig. 2.13 The Appointment Recurrence Dialogue Box.

The Calendar now shows the latest entry, including location

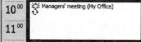

of meeting, together with the
Reminder icon, the **Recurring**
symbol, and the time span which
is surrounded in a blue line.

If you want to make any changes to the newly created

appointment, point to it and right-click it. You can use the options on this drop-down menu to print, edit, or delete the appointment. Choosing the **Edit Series** option, opens the Recurring Appointment dialogue box where you can make the required changes.

Next, let us now assume that you also have a special lunch appointment with your mother on the 4th of February each year, as it is her birthday. To enter this information click on 4 February on the calendar to the left of the Daily entry area, and create a yearly appointment 'Lunch with mother' for 1:00 p.m., for 1½ hours, as shown in Fig. 2.14 below. Add as a note the reminder 'Birthday lunch'.

Fig. 2.14 Entering a Yearly Appointment.

Note that the meeting with the Managers is also shown on the same day, as it is four weeks since the last meeting. This information also appears on the Weekly and the Monthly view. Try it!

Printing Information

Information held in a diary can be printed on paper. Simply use the **File**, **Print** command to open the dialogue box below.

Fig. 2.15 The Calendar Print Dialogue Box.

In the Printer **Name** box, at the top of the dialogue box, click the down arrow to select from one of the installed printers under Windows. Next, choose an appropriate item from the **Print style** list and use the **Page Setup** button to see the format, page size, and header/footer options of the selected print style.

In Fig. 2.16 on the next page, we show the Page Setup dialogue box with the Header/Footer tab selected. Note the five icon buttons below the Footer text boxes, also shown here. These can be used to insert page number, total number of pages, date, time, and user's name, respectively, in both headers and footers. To do so, simply place the insertion cursor on one of the text boxes, then click the appropriate button.

Fig. 2.16 Inserting a Footer in the Page Setup Dialogue Box.

In the above footer set-up, we have inserted the user's name in the left panel of the footer, the page number in the middle panel, and the date printed in the right panel. If you decide to show such information on your printout, it is entirely up to you where you choose to insert it. In addition, you can change the font type and font size of the information appearing on a header or footer.

If you want to change the font type and font size of the text appearing on the actual body of your printout, click the Format tab of the above dialogue box, and make appropriate selections under the displayed **Fonts** section. Pressing the **OK** button on the Page Setup dialogue box returns you to the Print dialogue box.

However, before committing anything to paper, use either the **Print Preview** button on the Setup dialogue box or the **Print** button on the Print dialogue box and save a few trees!

Planning a Meeting

Suppose we decide to invite other people into the meeting with the Managers on 7 January. First, locate the date of the meeting on the Calendar display and double-click the entry in question. In the displayed 'Open Recurring Item' screen, click the **Open this occurrence** radio button to display the Recurring Appointment dialogue box.

In this dialogue box, click the Scheduling tab to obtain the screen in Fig. 2.17, in which we typed the names of two colleagues we would like to be present at the meeting. If you had a Contacts list (see next section), you could also select one or more persons to attend this meeting by simply clicking the **Add Others** button on the dialogue box below and selecting from the displayed list.

Fig. 2.17 Scheduling Colleagues to Attend a Meeting.

From here, you can organise meetings and send requests to participants and then track the status of their response provided, of course, you are either connected to a local network or know their e-mail address. You can even give other Outlook users permissions to view your diary and to plan meetings with you at times when you are not so busy, but still be able to maintain private information in your diary.

Below we list several options available to Outlook 2003 on group Scheduling. However, these features require you to be using a Microsoft Exchange Server e-mail account.

- Ability to receive counter proposals for alternate meeting times. If allowed by the meeting organiser, invited colleagues can propose an alternate meeting time.

- Ability to view the schedules of multiple people or resources on a single calendar. The calendar contains a detailed graph of when each user is free and busy and also shows details of their appointments (except for those that they have marked private). When you rest the mouse pointer over an appointment, the details of that appointment are visible.

- Ability to use the Microsoft Office Internet Free/Busy Service to publish the blocks of time when you are free and when you are busy to a shared Internet location. This is convenient for people who don't normally have access to your Calendar but who do have Internet access. The service works with Microsoft Outlook so that the times published to the service also display in an Outlook meeting request when someone is trying to schedule a meeting with you. Anyone who isn't a member of the service and who you haven't specifically authorised to view your free/busy times won't be able to access the information you publish to the service. (The Microsoft Office Free/Busy Service requires the use of Microsoft Internet Explorer 5 or later.)

Other Outlook Facilities

Apart from 'Calendar', the other options on the Navigation Pane of Outlook contain all the elements needed to give you an effective time-management tool. These elements are accessed, as we have already seen, by appropriate buttons situated on the bottom left edge of the screen of the opening screen.

Contacts

The **Contacts** icon displays your contacts in a combined business card and list view. You can change the way information is displayed by clicking one of the **Current View** list formats. What is shown below is the Address Cards view format - you have the choice of six additional types of views.

Fig. 2.18 The Contacts Screen in Outlook.

To add a new contact, click the **New** button, shown here, or to edit an existing entry, double-click on the contact name. Either action displays a multi-tab dialogue box, shown in Fig. 2.19 on the next page, in which you type relevant information. We have only ever bothered to type details in the General tab sheet, but if you are so inclined, you can include someone's whole history by filling in the other tab sheets. Once this is done, the name, address, telephone numbers, and e-mail address from the General tab sheet are displayed in Outlook's Contact list. New to Outlook 2003 is the ability to add a photograph for each of your contacts by double-clicking the button pointed to in Fig. 2.19 and browsing to the folder that holds them.

Contact lists can be saved under different group names, so that you can have one list for your friends, and another for your business.

Fig. 2.19 Adding or Editing Contact Information.

The task of filling in such detailed information about an individual might be daunting at first, but you will find it very useful later. For example, you only have to left-click on the Web page address to be automatically connected to that Web page (of course, you will have to be connected to the Internet for that facility to work - see next chapter).

Equally, you could click on the phone icon on the toolbar to display the AutoDialer shown in Fig. 2.20. Pressing the **Start Call** button connects you to your contact via the modem, provided you have a voice capable modem and a handset or microphone attached to it.

Fig. 2.20 Using Outlook's AutoDialer Facility.

Tasks

Tasks can be displayed by clicking on the **Task** button of Outlook's Navigation Pane. Tasks are used to organise your personal to-do list, as well as keep track of your business. Tasks can be created by double-clicking on the area pointed to in Fig. 2.21 where we also show a list of personal tasks, with their due date of completion. Completed tasks are shown with a line through them.

Fig. 2.21 The Task List in Outlook.

Tasks can be assigned to other people within your organisation, and can help you keep track of progress on work that other people do for you or in co-operation with you. For example, you might assign a task to a colleague, or a colleague might assign a task to you in a group effort.

A task assignment requires at least two people: one to send a task request and another to respond to it. When you send a task request, you give up ownership of the task, but can keep an updated copy of it in your task list and receive status reports, but you cannot change information in it.

The person that receives the task request is the temporary owner of the task until acceptance of the task, in which case that person becomes the new, permanent owner of that task. Only temporary or permanent owners of a task can update that task. If a task is declined, ownership of the task is returned to the person who sent the task request.

To find out how to use the various functions appearing on a Tasks list, use the Outlook Help system and search for 'create tasks'. On the displayed list, first click the 'Create a Task' link then the 'Create a task from scratch' link pointed to in Fig. 2.22.

Fig. 2.22 Using the Outlook Help System.

Look through the various topics listed under the **Search Results** Pane of the above Help screen, and work through all of them. Using Help in this way, you will learn quickly how to sort and give priority to tasks, track task progress, enter recurring tasks once, assign tasks to others, and keep complex task lists organised.

Finally, try creating your own task list by either clicking the area under **Tasks** pointed to in Fig. 2.21, or clicking the **New** button shown here. Either of these actions displays a multi-tab dialogue box in which you type relevant information.

Journal

In Journal you can select to automatically record actions relating to specified contacts and to place the actions in a Timeline view. In addition to tracking Microsoft Outlook items, such as e-mail, or other Microsoft Office documents, such as Microsoft Word or Microsoft Excel files, you can keep a record of any interaction you want to remember, such as a telephone conversation or a letter you mailed or received.

Use Journal to record the dates and times of your interactions with contacts, such as tracking hours spent on a particular account. If you want to create a list of all the items related to a contact, use activity tracking, instead, to link the items to that contact.

To start Journal, use the **Go**, **Journal** command on the Outlook Menu Bar, to display the screen in Fig. 2.23.

Fig. 2.23 The Journal Options Dialogue Box.

To find out how to use the various functions appearing on a Journal list, use the Office Help system and search for 'Journal'. Go through all the displayed help options in a similar manner to that for Tasks. Try it, you will learn a lot.

3

E-mail with Outlook 2003

In what follows, it is assumed that your computer is capable of being connected to the Internet, or a local area network (LAN), so that you can receive e-mail. A connection to the Internet is usually made via a modem and a telephone line, an ethernet card to a LAN which itself is connected to the Internet, an ISDN direct line, or Broadband connection. The last two provide faster connection, but at present are more expensive than the alternatives.

Finally, you may also need to find, and possibly subscribe to, a suitable Internet Service Provider (ISP) which is a company that allows you to connect to its Internet host. There are many such providers in the UK. Most can be found in an Internet based PC magazine, your telephone directory, or possibly in adverts in one of the many computer magazines. Be careful though before committing yourself to one provider as the quality of service and costs can vary considerably. One thing we can't do here is make specific recommendations, but try and find someone who uses the company you decide on, or have a trial period with them.

All ISPs offer an e-mail address and mailbox facility to their customers; a mailbox being a storage area which holds your incoming messages until you connect to your ISP and download them to your computer so that you can read them. As long as your computer can access the Internet, you can use e-mail to keep in touch with friends and colleagues, anywhere in the world, provided they have their own e-mail address. The whole procedure of connecting to your ISP, downloading e-mail, filtering unwanted junk e-mail, saving and managing e-mail and other information, such as addresses of Web sites, can be done very easily in Outlook's e-mail facility - we will step you through the procedure later.

The Inbox Toolbar

You must have noticed by now that, apart from the symbols that appear on the screen of the various Outlook 2003 options, the buttons on the Toolbar also change from one option to the other. To see the ones below, first click the **Mail** button on the Navigation Pane, then select the **Inbox** option to display the **Inbox** toolbar buttons available before Outlook is configured for sending and receiving e-mail.

New Mail Message. Click the arrow to get ⇩

Print

Move to Folder

Delete

Reply

Reply to All

Forward

Find

Address Book

Office Help

Fig. 3.1 The New Menu Options.

Left-clicking an icon button can display a drop-down menu, (as shown in Fig. 3.1), action a command (such as displaying the Search Folder), or open an appropriate dialogue box so that you can, for example, search for items, such as mail flagged for follow-up.

Note that when you first open a drop-down menu similar to the one shown in Fig. 3.1, only the most frequently used options are visible. However, a few seconds later, or when you place the mouse pointer on the down-arrow appearing at the bottom of the menu, additional options are displayed. The latter are the less frequently used options, but once you select one, it joins the frequently used ones.

Modem Properties

If you are using a modem to connect to the Internet, you must check that Windows is configured correctly for this type of communication medium. Usually, after connecting your modem and starting your computer, Windows will auto-detect its presence using its Plug and Play capability.

To check that the modem is correctly configured, click the Windows *start* button and select **Control Panel** from the pop-up menu. This displays various Control Panel options from which you should double-click the **Phone and Modem Options** icon, shown here, to start the relevant program.

Windows will open the relevant dialogue box which we show on the left in Fig. 3.2 with its Modems tab selected. Click the **Properties** button, then select the Diagnostics tab and click the **Query Modem** button. If it displays the word 'success' your modem is working fine.

Fig. 3.2 Performing a Diagnostic Test on your Modem.

If in the Phone and Modem Options dialogue box the name of your actual modem is not displayed, then click the **Add** button to start the Install New Modem Wizard and follow the instructions on your screen.

The third Wizard screen is shown in Fig. 3.3 below. Windows displays a list of modems whose drivers are available to you.

Fig. 3.3 List of Modems by Manufacturer.

If your modem's Manufacturer or Modem does not appear on the displayed list, insert in your computer's appropriate drive the disc or CD that came with your modem and click the **Have Disk** button, as shown in Fig. 3.3. Finally, select the displayed modem driver and press the **OK** button to finish the installation.

Having installed your modem's driver it is a good idea to query the modem, following the procedure we discussed on the previous page, to make sure that it is recognised by Windows and it can communicate with it.

If you have any problems, click the **Properties** button on the Phone and Modem Options dialogue box, then click the **Troubleshoot** button on the displayed Modem Properties dialogue box and follow the instructions on the screen.

E-mail Settings

To configure Outlook 2003 to send and receive e-mail, use the **Tools, E-mail Accounts** command, as shown in Fig. 3.4, which starts the E-mail Accounts Wizard shown in Fig. 3.5.

Note: When the **Personal Folders** item under the **All Mail Folders** menu option is selected, Outlook 2003 displays, amongst other information, the **Tasks** you have to carry out. These were specified at the end of the previous Chapter.

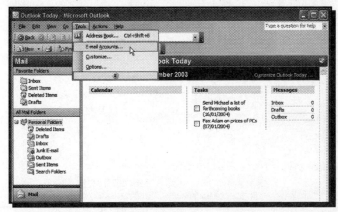

Fig. 3.4 The Mail Tools Drop-down Menu.

Fig. 3.5 The E-mail Accounts Wizard.

Returning to the job at hand, you can either edit previous accounts or create a new account from scratch. We choose here to **Add a new e-mail account**.

The second Wizard screen displays a list of types of server connections you could use for downloading your e-mail, such as Microsoft Exchange Server, POP3, IMAC, etc., and asks you to specify one. Our intended server type is a POP3 server, so after selecting it we clicked Next to display the third Wizard screen shown in Fig. 3.6.

Fig. 3.6 The E-mail Accounts Wizard.

Here, you must provide:

- Your name.

- Your e-mail address - this is supplied to you by your ISP when you join their services.

- The name of the 'Incoming' and 'Outgoing' mail server. This information is also supplied to you by your ISP.

- Your 'account name' and 'password' - again supplied to you by your ISP.

Next, and if you are using a phone line modem connection to the Internet, click the **More Settings** button, select the Connection tab and click the **Connect using my phone line** radio button shown in Fig. 3.7 on the next page.

Fig. 3.7 The Internet E-mail Settings.

This provides you with the ability to connect directly to your ISP whenever you want to use Outlook online, rather than having to first connect, then try to download your messages.

Finally, click the **OK** button to take you back to the dialogue box of Fig. 3.6, then click the **Test Account Settings** button. The Connect to your ISP dialogue box will then open and clicking the **Dial** button connects you to the Internet, verifies your user name and password and displays the dialogue box shown in Fig. 3.8.

Fig. 3.8 The E-mail Accounts Wizard.

If all the listed items are checked, then all is well. An automated message, generated by Outlook, is then sent to your **Inbox** to let you know that your settings are correct.

Closing this dialogue box and clicking the **Next** button, displays the final 'Congratulations' Wizard screen. Clicking the **Finish** button returns you to the screen of Fig. 3.4.

You are now in a position to send and receive e-mail. Note the appearance on Outlook's Toolbar of the **Send/Receive** button shown here. Provided you are still connected to the Internet, clicking this icon downloads any messages you might have waiting for you.

In our case Outlook downloaded 50 messages, 17 in our **Inbox** folder, and 33 in the **Junk mail** folder! Yes, we do receive an awful lot of junk mail, almost all from the USA. The decision on what goes in the **Junk mail** folder, shown in Fig. 3.9, was made automatically by Outlook.

Fig. 3.9 The Contents of the Junk Mail Folder.

This is a refreshing addition to Outlook's capabilities, and in the next section we will discuss the employment of additional rules to try and increase the rate of capture of junk mail. Having examined the mail in the **Junk mail** folder, we can vouch that all of it is in fact total junk. However, out of the 17 messages in our **Inbox**, only 4 were legitimate. This is because the Junk Mail Filter is set, by default, to 'low'.

Also by default, Outlook 2003 does not allow links to pictures on Websites in e-mail messages until the recipient has given their permission. This is because some spammers (people who send masses of unsolicited e-mail messages) use such pictures to prove to themselves that an e-mail address is alive.

Junk E-mail Folder Settings

To change the settings of the Junk E-mail folder, use the **Action**, **Junk E-mail** command, and select **Junk E-mail Options** from the drop-down sub-menu, as shown in Fig. 3.10 below.

Fig. 3.10 Selecting the Junk E-mail Options.

This opens the multi-tab dialogue box shown in Fig. 3.11.

Fig. 3.11 The Junk E-mail Options Dialogue Box.

As you can see, there is a lot to choose from here. In the Options tab-sheet you can select to have:

- No automatic filtering.

- Low filtering (the default setting).

- High filtering which might send some legitimate messages to the Junk E-mail folder (we found this setting excellent).

- Messages delivered to your Inbox only from people in your Safe List or Safe Recipient List.

For the latter option you must fill in either the Safe Senders tab-sheet, or the Safe Recipients tab-sheet. Such lists can be imported from pre-existing text files or added individually from the keyboard. You can also choose to have the names in your Contacts List as part of your Safe Senders List.

Creating E-mail Signatures

We are now ready to create an e-mail, but before we do so, we need to add to the configuration so that each e-mail you send shows your signature. Outlook 2003 allows each account holder to create a different signature which is an improvement on previous versions of the program.

To create a signature for all your outgoing e-mail messages, use the **Tools, Options** command, press the Mail Format tab of the displayed dialogue box, and click the **Signatures** button at the bottom of the Options dialogue box. This displays the Create Signature dialogue box shown partially obscured) in Fig. 3.12. Clicking the **New** button displays the Create New Signature Box. Give your signature a name, such as 'Signature 1', then press the **Next** button to open the Edit Signature dialogue box in which you can type what you want to appear at the bottom of each e-mail you send or forward.

It is only polite to supply your name and perhaps your e-mail address at the bottom of each electronic mail and make this the default signature for new and forwarded e-mail messages.

In addition, you could create another signature which could include your telephone number and/or your full address. In fact, you could create several signatures, each one with different content to be used depending on whether your e-mail is casual, formal, or professional, and switch between them as required. You can switch between signatures by highlighting the existing signature, right-clicking it to display a list of created signatures, and selecting an alternative.

Fig. 3.12 Creating E-mail Signatures.

However, before you finish with the Options dialogue box, make sure you choose one of the signatures for your new and forwarded e-mail messages, as shown below.

Creating and Sending E-mail

The best way to test out new e-mail features is to send a test message to your own e-mail address. This saves wasting somebody else's time, and the message can be very quickly 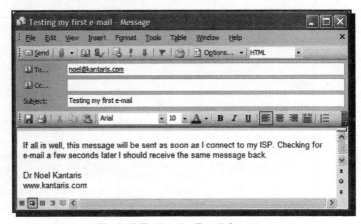 checked to see the results. So, click the **New** button to open the New Message dialogue box in which we compose the short message shown in Fig. 3.13.

Note the address in the **To...** box is shown underlined. This was automatically done by Outlook after we typed in the text string and moved to the **Subject:** box, because it is recognised as an e-mail address by Outlook. Later on we will discuss how to choose an address from the Address Book.

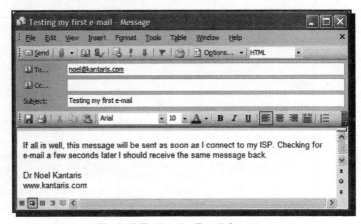

Fig. 3.13 Testing the E-mail System.

Each e-mail should have a short subject which is what will appear on the upper Inbox panel when the message is received by the recipient. The **Cc...** box is where you include the address of additional persons that you would like to receive a copy of the same message. To send the message, simply press the **Send** button which causes the New Message box to close down. What has happened here is that the message has been placed in Outlook's Outbox, waiting for you to perhaps compose another e-mail.

Fig. 3.14 Outlook's
List of Folders.

To see that your message is waiting in the Outbox, click on the **Personal Folders** to reveal all the mail folders, as shown in Fig. 3.14. As you can see, the **Outbox** folder is marked with one [1] item.

Should you want to edit a message in the Outbox, double-click its folder which opens an Outbox window listing all the messages held in it. Double-clicking one of these, opens the selected message ready for you to edit. Having edited a message, click the **Send** button again to place it back in the Outbox.

To send a message, click the **Send/Receive** button and follow the connection procedure to your ISP. Verification of what is happening is displayed at the bottom right corner of Outlook's window with the final message, shown here to the right, appearing for a very short time on the screen.

A few seconds later (sometimes longer), click again the **Send/Receive** button until the screen in Fig. 3.15 is revealed. This is the very message we sent a few seconds earlier which came back to us at the speed of light, well almost!

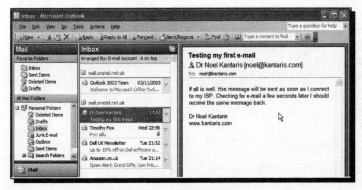

Fig. 3.15 An Incoming E-mail Message.

As you can see, the contents of a selected message in the Title Pane appear in Outlook's vertical Read Pane which has been redesigned to display more of your message than in previous versions of the program in which the message used to display in a horizontal pane. Double-clicking an e-mail title, opens the message in its own window, as shown in Fig. 3.16 below.

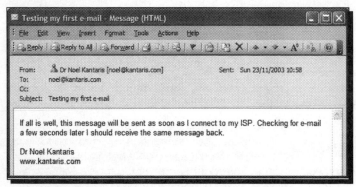

Fig. 3.16 An E-mail Opened in its Own Window.

Whether a message is opened in its own window or not, it could be transferred to a preselected folder, using the **Move to Folder** toolbar button. You could, for example, have a folder for each of the most important persons in your private or business life, thus keeping their messages together.

If you have received a message that you don't want to keep, then highlight it and press the **Delete** toolbar button. Deleted items are held in a folder, in case you want to resurrect them. To empty this folder, right-click the **Deleted Items** icon on Outlook's Folders Pane and select the **Empty "Deleted Items" Folder** option from the drop-down menu. To delete one item at a time, left-click it to select it, then either press the **Delete** button or the **Del** keyboard key. You will be asked to confirm deletion before the action is carried out.

A useful folder in which unfinished messages can be stored until they are ready to be sent, is the **Drafts** folder. We also use this folder to store our own message pro-formas.

Formatting your E-mail

Apart from sending messages in HTML (the default Hyper Text Markup Language used to format most documents on the Web), Outlook 2003 allows you to format your e-mail in Rich Text, or Plain Text. To select one of these, use the **Tools, Options** command and select the Mail Format tab to open the dialogue box in Fig. 3.17.

Fig. 3.17 The Mail Format Tab Screen of the Options Dialogue Box.

You can also select in the above dialogue box whether to use Microsoft Word as your default e-mail editor. Any of the above mentioned formats can be used with either Outlook or Word as your e-mail editor. Furthermore, you can use the **Actions, New Mail Message Using** command to create a single message in a format, or e-mail editor, other than the defaults that you have selected by choosing the message format or e-mail editor from the displayed menu shown in Fig. 3.18 on the next page.

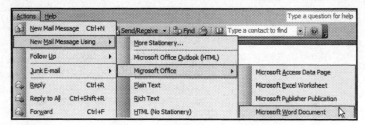

Fig. 3.18 The Actions, New Mail Message Using Cascade Menu.

However, remember that not everyone will be able to read the work you spent ages creating! There are still some people out there who use e-mail programs that are only capable of receiving plain text. So, it might be safer to avoid excessive text enhancements. The same can be said for Outlook's pre-formatted stationery under the HTML option.

Using E-mail Attachments

Sometimes, when you receive an e-mail with Outlook 2003, you might find at the bottom of the main text area, a file displayed, as shown in Fig. 3.19.

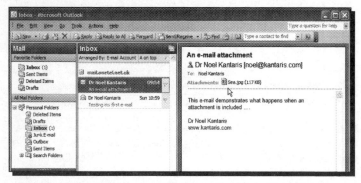

Fig. 3.19 The Display of an Attachment Received with an E-mail.

This indicates an attachment to the e-mail which can be a drawing, another formatted document, a photo, or even a sound and video file.

Until fairly recently, e-mail on the Internet was good only for short text notes. You could not send attachments like the ones mentioned above. That has now changed with the advent of MIME, which stands for Multipurpose Internet Mail Extension. With Outlook you can even send your favourite Web page as an attachment to an e-mail.

To view or save an attachment file, right-click its icon and choose to **Open**, or **Save As** from the drop-down menu. You can also view the attachment by double-clicking its icon.

Adding Attachments to your E-mail

If you want to include an attachment to your main e-mail message, you simply click the **Insert File** toolbar button shown here, and select the file to attach. This opens the Insert File dialogue box, for you to select the file, or files, you want to go with your message.

Before you start sending attachments with your e-mail, make sure that the person you are sending your message to has e-mail software capable of decoding them. In our experience some people seem to stick to their tried and trusted 'old' software that does not. If that is the case, only include one attachment per e-mail and mention in the text area of your e-mail what software you used to create the attachment; it will help the recipient to decipher it.

In Outlook 2003 the attached files are 'placed' below the **Subject** box, as shown in Fig. 3.20.

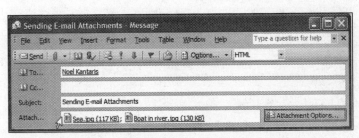

Fig. 3.20 Two Attachments Selected for Transmission.

Viewing and Sending Web Pages

To view Web pages using Outlook, use the **View**, **Toolbars** command and select the **Web** option from the drop-down menu. This displays the **Web** toolbar on the Outlook window (pointed to in Fig. 3.21). You can now use the Address box on this **Web** toolbar to view Web pages by typing in an appropriate Website address.

Fig. 3.21 Attaching a Web Page to an E-mail.

Even more interesting is the ease with which you can send a Web page as an e-mail. To do this, click the **Actions** menu command and select the **Send Web Page by E-Mail** option from the drop-down menu. This opens a New Mail Message screen, part of which is shown in Fig. 3.22, for you to type the

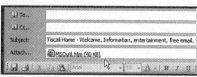

Fig. 3.22 An E-mail Attachment.

recipient's address. Outlook automatically includes a subject line which you can change, and the **Attachment** icon displayed below the Subject line. To preview such a file, double-click its attachment link (pointed to in Fig. 3.22).

Spell Checking

Some people do not seem to check their e-mail before clicking the **Send** button. With Outlook this could be avoided, as the program is linked to the spell checker that comes with Microsoft's Office. To try it out, prepare a message in the New Message window, but make an obvious spelling mistake, maybe like ours below. Pressing the **F7** function key, or using the **Tools**, **Spelling and Grammar** command, will start the process.

Fig. 3.23 Spell Checking an E-mail.

Any words not recognised by the spell checker will be flagged up as above. If you are happy with the word just click one of the **Ignore** buttons, if not, you can type a correction at the insertion point, or accept one of the **Suggestions**, and then click the **Change** button.

Selecting Options Settings

Now that we have finished experimenting with sending and receiving e-mail, it is a good idea to make some permanent changes to Outlook's settings. Use the **Tools, Options** command to open the Options dialogue box.

We suggest you make the following options selections:

- Click the Spelling tab and select the **Always check spelling before sending** option, so that every message you write is checked before it is sent.

- Click the Mail Setup tab and perhaps select **Hang up when finished with manual Send/Receive** option, so that you don't forget to disconnect your phone. Obviously, this setting assumes that your connection to the Internet is via a modem and phone line and you are paying for the call duration.

- Click the Other tab and check the **Empty the Deleted Items folder upon exiting** box.

- Click the Preferences tab and click the **E-mail Options** button which displays the E-mail Options dialogue box. In the **When replying to a message** and **When forwarding a message** list boxes you can select to include or not include the original message with your reply. If you choose to include it, make sure you edit it first - it is pointless making your reply longer by including the whole of the original message. If, on the other hand, you choose not to include it, make sure you refer to the points made in it; don't just answer 'yes' or 'no'. To implement any changes made in this dialogue box, click the **OK** button, which also returns you to the Options dialogue box.

Finally, to implement all the changes made in the Options dialogue box, click the **OK** button.

Obviously there are a lot more selections you could make, but we leave these to you. Very soon, after you have been using Outlook 2003 for a while, you will know yourself what options and preferences to choose.

Printing your Messages

It was originally thought by some, that computers would lead to the paperless office. That has certainly not proved to be the case, as most people want to see the results printed on paper. As far as information on software is concerned, long may it last!

Outlook 2003 lets you print to paper either lists of details of all e-mail messages in a selected folder (details being: who sent the e-mail, its subject, when it was received, and its size), or the actual contents of an e-mail.

To print a list of messages in a folder, select the folder, then use the **File**, **Print** command which displays the Print dialogue box shown in Fig. 3.24.

Fig. 3.24 The View Menu.

Choosing the **Table Style** from the **Print style** options, allows you to use the **Page Setup** option to select the size and font of both the column headings of your lists and their rows. You can also choose the paper size, and whether to add headers or footers to the tables before committing to paper.

Selecting the **Memo Style** (the default) for the **Print style** options in the Print dialogue box, sends the contents of the selected message to the printer.

Make sure the correct printer, page range, and number of copies you want are selected, then click the **OK** button. You can also start the printing procedure by clicking the Print toolbar icon shown here.

If the message has files attached to it and you want to print everything, then click the **Print attached files** box in the Print dialogue box to select it. However do note that attachments will print only to the default printer. For example, if you have printer A set as the default, and you open a message with an attachment and choose to print the e-mail to printer B, the message will be sent to printer B, but the attachment will go to printer A. So, if you have two printers, one black and white and one colour, and you want to print the attachments in colour make sure you assign the colour printer as the default.

The Address Book

E-mail addresses are often quite complicated and not at all easy to remember. With Outlook there is a very useful Address Book built in and accessed by clicking the menu icon with the same name. Below in Fig. 3.25, we show part of an example.

Fig. 3.25 The Address Book Screen.

Once in the Address Book, you can manually add a person's full details and e-mail address, in the Properties box that opens when you click the **New Entry** toolbar icon (pointed to in Fig. 3.26) and select **New Contact** in the displayed New Entry dialogue box.

Fig. 3.26 Creating a New Contacts Entry

Clicking the **OK** button, displays the yet untitled Properties dialogue box shown in Fig. 3.27 below.

Fig. 3.27 The New Contacts Property Dialogue Box.

Typing a contact's name in the **Full Name** text box renames the Properties dialogue box with that name which can then be saved using the **Save and Close** toolbar button.

To make a viable e-mail Contacts list, you only need to fill in the **Full Name**, **File as**, **E-mail**, and **Display as** entries in the Properties dialogue box. However, you could make this your full contacts list as we saw earlier on page 40 in Chapter 2.

Outlook allows you to access e-mail addresses from either the Address Book/Contacts list or the Global Address Book list. However, the latter requires you to be using a Microsoft Exchange Server e-mail account and its list contains the names and e-mail addresses of everyone in your organisation. The Microsoft Exchange Server administrator is the only person that can create and maintain this address book.

If you have been using Outlook Express as your e-mail application and now you want to switch to Outlook 2003, you can import all your e-mail addresses from your previous Address Book into the Address Book/Contacts list by using the **File**, **Import and Export** menu command on the Outlook Today window. This starts the Outlook Import and Export Wizard where you can specify in successive screens to:

- Import Internet Mail and Addresses.

- Import from Eudora or Outlook Express, e-mail messages, Address Book entries, and e-mail rules.

- Allow replacement of existing entries, or allow duplicates to be created.

Allowing duplicates to be created might be a better option here, particularly if you have already imported data into Contacts from another Personal Organiser - you can always tidy up such duplicate entries later. Once all choices have been made, the Wizard transfers all the specified data and creates a complete list of Contacts which you can use to send e-mail messages. Important e-mail messages are also transferred from your old e-mail program into appropriate folders in Outlook 2003.

To send a new message to anyone listed in your Address Book/Contacts list, open a New Message window and click on any of the **To:** or **Cc:** icons shown here on the left.

In the Select Names box which is opened (Fig. 3.28), you can select a person's name and click either the **To->** button to place it in the **To** field of your message, the **Cc->** button to place it in the **Cc** field, or the **Bcc->**button to place it in the **Bcc** field.

Fig. 3.28 The Select Names Screen.

Note: Cc is an abbreviation for carbon copy. If you add a recipient's name to this box in a message, a copy of the message is sent to that recipient, and the recipient's name is visible to other recipients of the message.

Bcc is an abbreviation for blind carbon copy. If you add a recipient's name to this box in a message, a copy of the message is sent to that recipient, and the recipient's name is not visible to other recipients of the message. The **Bcc** field becomes visible in a New Outlook message when you add recipients to the corresponding field in Fig. 3.28.

* * *

In the last two chapters, we have tried to cover sufficient information on Outlook 2003, so that you can get to grips with the program and get on with the job of sending and receiving e-mail effectively, being one of the most used activities on the Internet.

Outlook has many more features, far too numerous to discuss in the space allocated here. What we have tried to do, is give you enough basic information so that you can have the confidence to explore the rest of Outlook's capabilities by yourself. Have fun!

* * *

4

Microsoft Word 2003 Basics

Microsoft's Word 2003 is part of the Office 2003 package and is without doubt the best Windows word processor so far. As you would expect, it is fully integrated with all the other Office 2003 applications. This version of Word, like its predecessors, has particularly strong leanings towards desk top publishing which offers fully editable WYSIWYG (what you see is what you get) modes that can be viewed in various zoom levels. Couple this with the ability to include and manipulate full colour graphics and to easily create Web pages and you can see the enormous power of the program. You will find using Word 2003 to be even more intuitive and easy than earlier versions and you will soon be producing the type of word processed output you would not have dreamt possible.

In many situations Word 2003 will attempt to anticipate what you want to do and will probably produce the correct result most of the time. For example, AutoCorrect and AutoFormat can, when active, correct common spelling mistakes and format documents automatically. Other Wizards can help you with everyday tasks and/or make complex tasks easier to manage.

Word uses Object Linking and Embedding (OLE) to move and share information seamlessly between Office 2003 applications. For example, you can drag information from one application to another, or you can link information from one application into another. Similarly, Hyperlinks can be used from any of the Office 2003 applications to access other Office documents, files on an internal or external Web or FTP (File Transfer Protocol) site, or HTML (Hypertext Markup Language) files. Hyperlinks help you use your documents with the Internet.

Starting the Word Program

Word is started in Windows either by clicking the *start* button then selecting **All Programs**, **Microsoft Office** and clicking 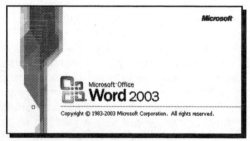 on the **Microsoft Word** icon on the cascade menu, or by double-clicking on a Word document file. In the latter case the document will be loaded into Word at the same time.

When you start Word the program momentarily displays its opening screen, (Fig. 4.1), and then displays the first page of a new document, shown in Fig. 4.2 - more about this shortly.

Fig. 4.1 Word's Opening Screen.

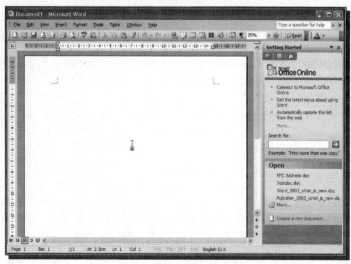

Fig. 4.2 Word's New Document Screen.

Whether you have used a previous version of Word or not, the first time you use the program, it might be a good idea to click the **Microsoft Office Word Help** button on the toolbar, then click the **Table of Contents** link on the Help Task Pane. This displays a list of help books, and clicking the first one opens a list of help topics as shown in Fig. 4.3 below.

Clicking the 'What's new in Microsoft Office Word 2003' help topic, opens a separate Help window with a list of additional topics. As you click each hypertext link, Word Help displays several topics on the subject. After looking at these options, have a look at the other options displayed in the Help Pane. We suggest you spend a little time here browsing through the various topics before going on.

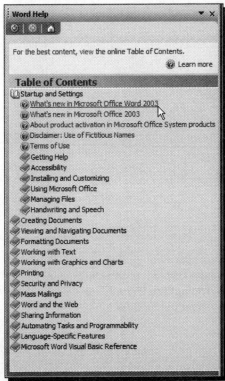

Fig. 4.3 The Microsoft Word Help Screen.

The Word Screen

The opening 'blank' screen of Word 2003 is shown below. It is perhaps worth spending some time looking at the various parts that make up this screen. Word follows the usual Microsoft Windows conventions and if you are familiar with these you can skip some of this section, but even so, a few minutes might be well spent here.

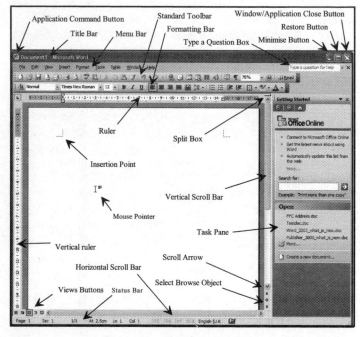

Fig. 4.4 The Word Screen Layout.

The above screen differs slightly from that of Fig. 4.1; for clarity we have moved the Formatting bar below the Standard toolbar - more about this shortly.

The layout, as shown, is in a window, but if you click on the application Restore button, you can make Word take up the full screen area available. Using a window can be useful when you are running several applications at the same time and you want to transfer between them with the mouse.

For an explanation of Word's screen areas, please refer to Appendix A, and for the menu bar options and Task Panes refer to Appendix B.

Note that in this case, the Word window displays an empty document with the title 'Document1', and has a solid 'Title bar', indicating that it is the active application window. Although multiple windows can be displayed simultaneously, you can only enter data into the active window (which will always be displayed on top, unless you view them on a split screen). Title bars of non-active windows appear a lighter shade than that of the active one.

The Toolbars

There are twenty different toolbars available in Word 2003. To see the full list you can use the **View**, **Toolbars** menu command, or more easily, right-click in the toolbar area. In this list active bars are shown with a ticked orange square to their left. Clicking on a list entry will toggle that toolbar on or off. By default, only three bars are active, the Standard, the Formatting, and the Task Pane.

When Word is first opened the first two bars will probably be placed alongside each other, which means that not all the buttons will be visible. To see the other available buttons click the toolbar options button pointed to in Fig. 4.5.

Fig. 4.5 Toolbar Options.

Clicking any of the displayed buttons will action that function. For our screen layout of Fig. 4.4 we have clicked the **Show Buttons on Two Rows** option. We find it easier to work with both toolbars almost fully open.

Do note that Word automatically customises both toolbars and menus, based on how often you use their commands. As you work, they adjust so that only the buttons and commands you use most often are shown. Thus your screen may not display the same features as ours.

The Standard Toolbar

As we show it, this is located below the Menu bar at the top of the Word screen and contains command buttons. As you move the mouse pointer over a button it changes to an 'active' blue colour and a banner opens to indicate the button's function. Left-clicking the button will then action that function or command.

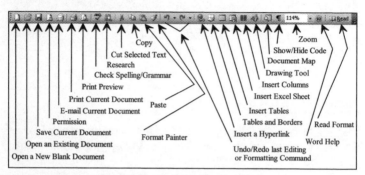

Fig. 4.6 Standard Toolbar Functions.

Most of the Standard toolbar buttons will be discussed in the following sections of the book. However, the **Read** format button, is new to this version of Word. Using this Layout View allows you to easily read documents on screen rather than having to print them out.

The **Read** view uses a new, ClearType, technology and large fonts to make screen reading a lot more comfortable, as shown in Fig. 4.7, hence what you see on screen is not the same as what will print on paper. A document in this view is displayed in a separate window and has the appearance of a book - you can even turn pages on screen as you would when reading a book!

The Read Layout View is used automatically when opening e-mail attachments that used Word when composing them. If you don't like this view, you could always turn it off by using the **Tools**, **Options** menu command and clearing the tick box against the **Allow starting in Reading Layout** option.

Fig. 4.7 The Read View Screen Format.

The view above is that of the introductory pages of this book, in fact page viii. Yet in the Read view format, the original page appears as pages 13 and 14. The total number of pages in this new format depends on the size of the window in which you are viewing them.

The buttons at the bottom right of the window of Fig. 4.7, shown enlarged here, can be used to go to the **Previous Page**, **Select Browse Object**, or go to the **Next Page**. Clicking the **Select Browse Object** button reveals a list of objects, shown here, that you can use to browse your document. For example, you can browse by Page (going from one page to the next, by Section (going from one section to the next), or by Picture going from one picture to the next), to mention but a few. To see which option is which, place the mouse pointer on an object and its function will replace the **Cancel** button.

The Formatting Bar

This is located to the right of, or below, the Standard Toolbar, and is divided into sections that contain command buttons, as shown in Fig. 4.8 below.

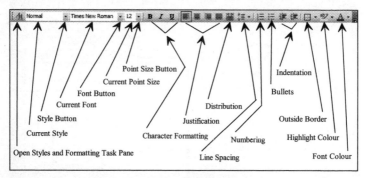

Fig. 4.8 Formatting Toolbar Functions.

The first option displays the name of the current style (Normal) in a box. Clicking the down-arrow against this box, opens up a menu of default paragraph styles with their font sizes. The Current font box shows the current typeface. Clicking on the down-arrow button to the right of it allows you to change the typeface of any selected text. The Current point size box shows the size of selected characters which can be changed by clicking on the down-arrow button next to it and selecting another size from the displayed list.

Next, are three character formatting buttons which allow you to enhance selected text by emboldening, italicising, or underlining it. The next ten buttons allow you to change the justification of a selected paragraph, control character distribution, control line spacing and set the different types of numbering, bullet, and indentation options. The last three buttons allow you to add an Outside Border to selected text or objects, and change the highlight and font colour of selected text.

The Status Bar

This is located at the bottom of the Word window and is used to display statistics about the active document.

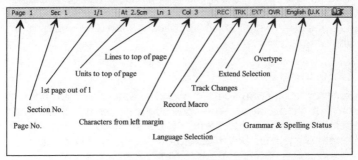

Fig. 4.9 The Word Status Bar.

For example, when a document is being opened, the Status bar displays for a short time its name and length in terms of total number of characters. Once a document is opened, the Status bar displays the statistics of the document at the insertion point; here it is on Page 1, Section 1, and 3 characters from the left margin.

Double-clicking the left of the status bar displays the Find and Replace dialogue box, as shown in Fig. 4.10. This is shown with the **Go To** tab selected. You can choose which page, section line, etc., of the document to go to, or you can use the other tabs to **Find** and **Replace** text (more about this later). Double-clicking the other features on the Status bar will also activate their features.

Fig. 4.10 The Find and Replace Box.

Creating Word Documents

When the program is first used, all Word's features default to those shown in Fig. 4.4. It is quite possible to use Word in this mode, without changing any main settings, but obviously it is possible to customise the package to your needs, as we shall see later.

Entering Text

In order to illustrate some of Word's capabilities, you need to have a short text at hand. We suggest you type the memo below into a new document. At this stage, don't worry if the length of the lines below differ from those on your display.

As you type in text, any time you want to force a new line, or paragraph, just press <Enter>. While typing within a paragraph, Word sorts out line lengths automatically (known as 'word wrap'), without you having to press any keys to move to a new line.

MEMO TO PC USERS
Data Processing Computers
The microcomputers in the Data Processing room are a mixture of IBM compatible PCs with Pentium processors running at various speeds. They all have 3.5" floppy drives of 1.44MB capacity, some with CD-ROM drives, and some with DVD drives. The PCs are connected to various printers, including a couple of colour printers, via a network; the Laser printers giving best output.

The computer you are using will have at least a 30GB capacity hard disc on which a number of software programs, including the latest version of Microsoft Windows and Microsoft Office, have been installed. To make life easier, the hard disc is partitioned so that data can be kept separate from programs. The disc partition that holds the data for the various applications running on the computer is highly structured, with each program having its own folder in which its own data can be held.

Fig. 4.11 A Short Memo to Illustrate Word's Capabilities.

Moving Around a Document

You can move the cursor around a document with the normal direction keys, and with the key combinations listed below.

To move	*Press*
Left one character	←
Right one character	→
Up one line	↑
Down one line	↓
Left one word	Ctrl+←
Right one word	Ctrl+→
To beginning of line	Home
To end of line	End
To paragraph beginning	Ctrl+↑
To paragraph end	Ctrl+↓
Up one screen	PgUp
Down one screen	PgDn
To top of previous page	Ctrl+PgUp
To top of next page	Ctrl+PgDn
To beginning of file	Ctrl+Home
To end of file	Ctrl+End

Fig. 4.12 Page Change Controls.

To move to a specified page number in a multi-page document, either drag the vertical scroll bar up or down until the required page number is shown, as in Fig. 4.12, or use the **Edit**, **Go To** command (or <Ctrl+G>), as described on page 79.

To easily step from page to page you can also click the **Previous Page** ▓ and **Next Page** ▓ buttons, shown in Fig. 4.12.

Obviously, you need to become familiar with these methods of moving the cursor around a document, particularly if you spot an error in a document which needs to be corrected, which is the subject of the latter half of this chapter.

Templates and Paragraph Styles

As we saw under the Formatting Bar section earlier, when you start Word for the first time, the Style box contains the word **Normal**. This means that all the text you have entered, at the moment, is shown in the Normal paragraph style which is one of the styles available in the NORMAL template. Every document produced by Word has to use a template, and NORMAL is the default. A template contains both the document page settings and a set of formatting instructions which can be applied to text.

To change the style of a paragraph, first open the **Styles and Formatting** Task Pane by clicking its toolbar button, as shown here. Place the cursor in the paragraph in question, say the title line and select the **Heading 1** style from the **Pick formatting to apply** list in the Task Pane. The selected paragraph reformats instantly in bold, and in Arial typeface of point size 16.

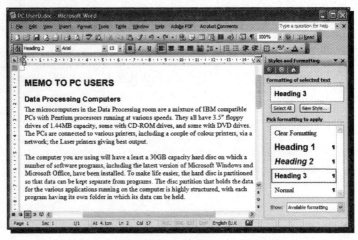

Fig. 4.13 Using the Styles and Formatting Task Pane.

Now with the cursor in the second line of text, select **Heading 3** which reformats the line in Arial 13. Your memo should now look presentable, and be similar to Fig. 4.13 above.

The other way of setting these styles is from the Style box on the Word Formatting toolbar, as shown here in Fig. 4.14.

Fig. 4.14 Using the Style Box.

If you try both methods you will find that in the long run the Task Pane method is better. As we shall see later, you can carry out most, if not all, of your style format work from the Task Pane without having to resort to dialogue boxes. This makes the various features of Word more accessible, which is to be welcomed.

However, the body of the memo is in Times New Roman typeface of point size 12, which is also the definition of the **Normal** style. Later on we will discuss how to also change this to Arial, so as to avoid having a mixture of typefaces.

Document Screen Displays

Word provides five display views, **Normal**, **Web Layout**, **Print Layout**, **Reading Layout** and **Outline**, as well as the options to view your documents in a whole range of screen enlargements by selecting **Zoom**. You control all these viewing options with the **View** sub-menu, shown in Fig. 4.15, and when a document is displayed you can switch freely between them. When first loaded the screen displays in **Print Layout** view.

The main view options have the following effect, and can also be accessed by clicking the **Views** buttons on the left of the Status bar at the bottom of the Word window (see Fig. 4.4).

Fig. 4.15 View Menu.

Normal Layout

A view that simplifies the layout of the page so that you can type, edit and format text quickly. In normal view, page boundaries, headers and footers, backgrounds, drawing objects, and pictures that do not have the **'In line with text'** wrapping style do not appear.

Web Layout

A view that optimises the layout of a document to make online reading easier. Use this layout view when you are creating a Web page or a document that is viewed on the screen. In Web layout view, you can see backgrounds, text is wrapped to fit the window, and graphics are positioned just as they are in a Web browser.

Print Layout

Provides a WYSIWYG (what you see is what you get) view of a document. The text displays in the typefaces and point sizes you specify, and with the selected attributes.

This view is useful for editing headers and footers, for adjusting margins, and for working with columns and drawing objects. All text boxes or frames, tables, graphics, headers, footers, and footnotes appear on the screen as they will in the final printout.

Reading Layout

Provides an easy to read view of a document. The text displays in a new, ClearType, technology and large typefaces to make screen reading a lot more comfortable, but what you see on the screen is not what will print on paper.

Outline Layout

Provides a collapsible view of a document, which enables you to see its organisation at a glance. You can display all the text in a file, or just the text that uses the paragraph styles you specify. Using this mode, allows you to quickly rearrange large sections of text.

Some people like to create an outline of their document first, consisting of all the headings, then sort out the document structure and finally fill in the text.

With large documents, you can create what is known as a master document by starting with an Outline View, and then designating headings in the outline as sub-documents. When you save the master document, Word assigns names to each sub-document based on the text you use in the outline headings.

Document Map

This view displays a separate pane with a list of document headings. You can quickly navigate through the document, when you click a heading Word jumps to that place in the document and displays the heading at the top of the window.

Full Screen

Selecting the **View, Full Screen** command, displays a clean, uncluttered screen; the Toolbars, Ruler, Scroll bars, and Status bar are removed. To return to the usual screen, click the **Close Full Screen** button on the icon which appears on your screen when in this mode.

Changing Word's Default Options

Modifying Margins

It is easy to change the standard page margins for your entire document from the cursor position onward, or for selected text (more about this later).

Select the **File, Page Setup** command, click the left mouse button on the **Margins** tab of the displayed dialogue box, shown in Fig. 4.16 below, and change any of the margin or gutter settings in the **Margins** boxes.

Fig. 4.16 Margins Sheet of the Page Setup Box.

The **Preview** page at the bottom of the box shows how your changes will look on a real page. The orientation of the printed page is normally **Portrait** where text prints across the page width, but you can change this to **Landscape** which prints across the page length, if you prefer.

Changing the Default Paper Settings

To change the default paper settings from those set during installation you do the following.

As before, select the **File, Page Setup** command, but click the **Paper** tab on the Page Setup dialogue box. Click the down-arrow against the **Paper size** box to reveal the list of available paper sizes, as shown in Fig. 4.17. Change the page size to your new choice.

Fig. 4.17 Paper Sheet of the Page Setup Box.

Any changes you can make to your document from the Page Setup dialogue box can be applied to either the whole document or to the rest of the document starting from the current position of the insertion pointer. To set this, click the down-arrow button against the **Apply to** box and choose from the drop-down list. To make any of the new settings 'permanent', press the **Default** button and confirm that you wish this change to affect all new documents based on the Normal template.

The Paper source section of the Page Setup box lets you set where your printer takes its paper from. You might have a printer that holds paper in trays, in which case you might want to specify that the **First page** (headed paper perhaps), should be taken from one tray, while **Other pages** should be taken from a different tray.

Modifying the Page Layout

Clicking the Page Setup tab displays the Layout box, part of which is shown here. From this dialogue box you can set options for headers and footers, section breaks, vertical alignment and whether to add line numbers or borders.

Fig. 4.18 Layout Sheet of the Page Setup Box.

The default for **Section Start** is 'New Page' which allows the section to start at the top of the next page. Pressing the down arrow against this option, allows you to change this choice.

In the Headers and Footers section of the dialogue box, you can specify whether you want one header or footer for even-numbered pages and a different header or footer for odd-numbered pages. You can further specify if you want a different header or footer on the first page from the header or footer used for the rest of the document. Word aligns the top line with the 'Top' margin, but this can be changed with the **Vertical alignment** option.

Changing Other Default Options

You can also change the other default options available to you in Word 2003, by selecting the **Tools, Options** command. This opens the Options dialogue box displayed in Fig. 4.19 below.

Fig. 4.19 The Word Options Dialogue Box.

As can be seen, this box has eleven tabbed sheets which give you control of most of the program's settings.

You can, amongst other things, do the following:

- Specify the default **View** options. For example, you can select whether non-printing formatting characters, such as Tabs, Spaces, and Paragraph marks, are shown.

- Adjust the **General** Word settings, such as background re-pagination, display of the recently used file-list, and selection of units of measurement.

- Adjust the **Print** settings, such as allowing background printing, reverse print order, or choose to print comments with documents.

- Change the **Save** options, such as selecting to always create a backup copy of your work.

Saving to a File

To save a document to disc, use either of the commands:

- **File, Save** (or click the **Save** toolbar button) which is used when a document has previously been saved to disc in a named file; using this command saves your work under the existing filename automatically without prompting you.

- **File, Save As** command which is used when you want to save your document with a different name from the one you gave it already.

Using the **File, Save As** command (or with the very first time you use the **File, Save** command when a document has no name), opens the dialogue box shown in Fig. 4.20.

Note that the first 255 characters of the first paragraph of a new document are placed and highlighted in the **File name** field box, with the program waiting for you to over-type a new name.

Any name you type must have less than 255 characters and will replace the existing name. Filenames cannot include any of the following keyboard characters: /, \, >, <, *, ?, ", |, :, or ;. Word adds the file extension **.doc** automatically and uses it to identify its documents.

Fig. 4.20 The File Save As Box.

You can select a drive other than the one displayed, by clicking the down arrow against the **Save in** text box at the top of the Save As dialogue box. You can also select a folder in which to save your work. The large buttons on the left of the box give rapid access to five possible saving locations. If you do not have a suitably named folder, then you can create one using the **Create New Folder** button, as shown below.

Fig. 4.21 Creating a New Folder.

We used this facility to create a folder called **Office 2003 Docs** within the **Documents** folder. To save our work currently in memory, we selected this folder in the **Save in** field of the Save As dialogue box, then moved the cursor into the **File name** box, and typed **PC User1**. We suggest you do the same. The name currently displayed in the box is the title of our memo which Word suggests as a suitable filename.

By clicking the **Save as type** button at the bottom of the Save As dialogue box, you can save the Document Template, or the Text Only parts of your work, or you can save your document in a variety of 10 formats, including Rich Text, and several Web Page options.

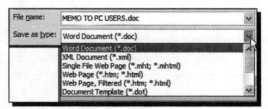

Fig. 4.22 Saving a Document as a Different File Type.

Selecting File Location

You can select where Word automatically looks for your document files when you first choose to open or save a document, by selecting the **Tools, Options** command, clicking the File Locations tab of the displayed Options dialogue box, (Fig. 4.19), and modifying the location of the document files, as shown on the next page in Fig. 4.23. As you can see, the default location of other types of files is also given in this dialogue box.

Microsoft suggests that you store documents, worksheets, presentations, databases, and other files you are currently working on, in the **My Documents** folder, which is easily accessed from the Desktop by clicking the special **Documents** button. This, of course, is a matter of preference, so we leave it to you to decide. We prefer to create sub-folders within **My Documents** to group our files more closely.

Fig. 4.23 Setting Word's File Locations.

To change the default folder for any of the file types listed above, simply select the type and click the **Modify** button. This opens a dialogue box very similar to the Save As box for you to locate or even create the folder you want to select.

While any of the file opening, saving and location dialogue boxes are open you can use them to generally manage your files and folders. You do this by right-clicking on the name of a file or folder you want to manipulate. A context sensitive menu is opened like ours in Fig. 4.24. All of these options may not be available on your system, but the common ones of Open, New, Print, Cut, Copy, Create Shortcut, Delete, Rename and Properties should always be there.

Fig. 4.24 The File Right-click Menu.

Document Properties

A useful feature in Word is the facility to add document properties to every file by selecting the **File, Properties** command. A Properties box, as shown in Fig. 4.25 below, opens for you to type additional information about your document.

Fig. 4.25 The Document Properties Box.

One of the most useful features in this box is the Statistics tabbed page. As we show in Fig. 4.26, this gives a listing of the document statistics, including the number of pages, paragraphs, lines, words and even characters. Very useful for writing papers and reports, where the size is important.

Statistic name	Value
Pages:	1
Paragraphs:	4
Lines:	14
Words:	152
Characters:	753
Characters (with spaces):	902

Fig. 4.26 Document Statistics.

To use this feature on a more regular basis, make sure that the **Prompt for document properties** box appears ticked on the Save tabbed sheet of the Options dialogue box (use the **Tools, Options** command and click the Save tab).

Closing a Document

There are several ways to close a document in Word. Once you have saved it you can click its ⊠ close button, or double-click on the **Document Control** button at the left end of the menu bar, or use the **File, Close** menu command.

If the document (or file) has changed since the last time it was saved, you will be given the option to save it before it is removed from memory.

If a document is not closed before a new document is opened, then both documents will be held in memory, but

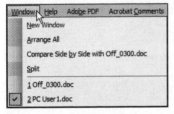

only one will be the current document. To find out which documents are held in memory, look at the Windows Taskbar, (see note below) or use the **Window** command to reveal the menu options shown in Fig. 4.27.

Fig. 4.27 Window Menu.

In this case, the second document in the list is the current document, and to make another document the current one, either type the document number, or point at its name and click the left mouse button.

To close a document which is not the current document, use the **Window** command, make it current, and close it with one of the above methods.

Note - With Word 2003 it is possible to limit what is shown on the Taskbar. By default all your open Word windows (or documents) will each have an entry on the Taskbar. But you can change this so that only the current, or active, document is shown there. This can be useful to save clutter if you have several programs open at the same time.

To do this, open the View tab sheet of the **Tools, Options** dialogue box, shown in Fig. 4.19, and uncheck the **Windows in Taskbar** option.

Opening a Document

You can use the Open dialogue box in Word, shown in Fig. 4.28 below, to open documents that might be located in different locations. As we saw earlier, this is opened by clicking the **Open** toolbar button, or with the **File**, **Open** command, or the <Ctrl+O> keystrokes.

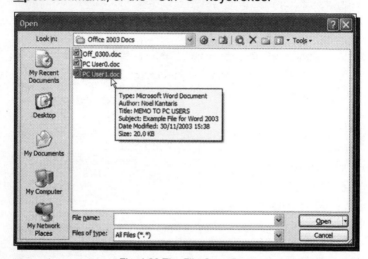

Fig. 4.28 The File Open Box.

For example, you can open a document which might be on your computer's hard disc, or on a network drive that you have a connection to. To locate other drives and folders, simply click the **Up One Level** button pointed to in Fig. 4.29 below.

Fig. 4.29 The Up One Level Button.

Having selected a drive, you can then select the folder within which your document was saved, select its filename and click the **Open** button on the dialogue box.

As in older versions of Word, the last few files you worked on are also listed at the bottom of the **File** menu, as shown in Fig. 4.30 below. Selecting one of these will reopen that file.

If you do not have any past files displayed, as described above, open the General tab sheet of the **Tools**, **Options** dialogue box, and make sure the **Recently used file list** option is checked. In the **entries** box next to it you can choose to have up to the last nine files listed. The default is four, which is probably plenty for most people.

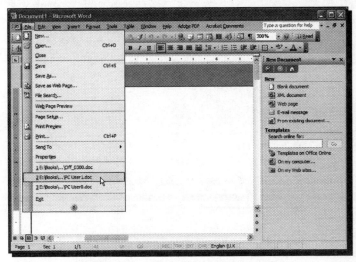

Fig. 4.30 Opening the Last Used Documents.

The New Document Task Pane

The **New Document** Task Pane, shown above, is another way of opening various types of documents. If it is not open, simply use the **View**, **Task Pane** command, then select it from the **Task** Pane drop-down options.

Under the **New** section you can open a **Blank document** using the Normal template (the same as clicking the **New** toolbar button), a blank **XML document**, a blank **Web page**, a blank **E-mail message**, or a new document based on the features of an existing one.

The **Templates** section lets you open a template to use for your document. Microsoft have produced 'hundreds' of templates for particular types of documents. These make it very easy for a 'newish' user to produce very professional documents. Once opened you just change the existing text to your own, print it and wait for the admiring comments - maybe. The **On my computer** option accesses those that came with Word, as shown in Fig. 4.31.

Fig. 4.31 Some of the Templates Available in Word.

These templates are well worth exploring as you may save yourself an awful lot of work. Templates provide you with instructions suggesting how to customise them. Once you have found the template you like and have entered your name and address, it is a good idea to save the document again, but as a template, so that you can use it again in the future. To do this, select Document Template in the **Save as type** box of the Save As dialogue box and rename the document. It will then be available in the General tabbed section of the Templates box for your use.

The other two template options on the **New** section of the **New Document** Task Pane let you access templates from your own Web space, maybe a company intranet, or from Microsoft's own Web sites. That should keep you busy for a while!

5

Editing Word Documents

Microsoft have built some very clever editing facilities into Word 2003, and we will introduce some of them here. When you enter text you will notice that some basic errors are automatically corrected and that misspelled words are unobtrusively underlined in a red wavy line and ungrammatical phrases are similarly underlined in green.

AutoCorrect

To demonstrate these, use the **File, New** command (or click ⬜) to create a new file, and type the words 'teh computor is brukn', exactly as misspelled here.

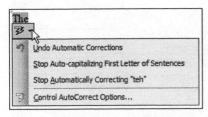

Fig. 5.1 The AutoCorrect Option Button.

As soon as you press the space bar after entering the first 'word', it will be changed to 'The', as shown in Fig. 5.1. This is the **AutoCorrect** feature at work, which will automatically detect and correct typing errors, misspelled words, and incorrect capitalisation. If you agree with the change made, as in our example, all is well. If not, you can move the pointer over the corrected word until a blue box is shown below it. This changes to the **AutoCorrect Options** button when you point to it, and clicking it opens the menu shown above.

Selecting the first menu option **Undo Automatic Corrections** will cancel the correction for you. The other options give you control of how the feature works in the future.

What should appear on your screen is shown in Fig. 5.2, with the two misspelled words underlined in a red wavy line.

Fig. 5.2 Correcting Spelling Mistakes.

Right-clicking the first misspelled word allows you to correct it, as shown above. To do this, left-click the **Computer** menu option. You even have a choice of **Language** to use. This is possibly the most timesaving enhancement in editing misspelled words as you type.

During this process the status bar will indicate your 'state of play'. As shown in Fig. 5.3, the active language is displayed, English (UK) in our case. To the right of this, the small 'book' icon has

Fig. 5.3 The Status Bar.

three forms. In Fig. 5.3 it is ticked to indicate that spell checking is completed. If there are errors to correct, it has a red cross on it, and during the actual checking process it displays an active pencil as shown here to the left. If you double-click this icon when it displays a cross, the full spell and grammar checker is opened which will be discussed later in more detail.

If you really have a problem spelling particular words you can add them to the AutoCorrect list yourself. To do this, select the **AutoCorrect** option from the menu in Fig. 5.2 (or the **Tools**, **AutoCorrect Options** menu command) to open the AutoCorrect box shown in Fig. 5.4 on the next page.

Fig. 5.4 Controlling AutoCorrections.

This dialogue box lets you control all of Word's automatic text, formatting and correction features, as well as the new Smart Tags feature we will encounter later on. Make sure the AutoCorrect tabbed sheet is active, as shown above, and have a good look at the ways you can control how it works for you. We suggest you scroll through the very long list of common misspellings at the bottom to see which ones will automatically be corrected.

In our example we have chosen to have the program always **Replace** the word 'computor' **With** the correct spelling of 'computer' as soon as we type the word. Clicking the **Add** button will add these to the AutoCorrect list.

The top fifteen options on the list are not corrections, but give you a rapid way to enter some common symbol characters by typing in a series of keyboard strokes. For example, if you type the three characters '(c)' AutoCorrect will change them to the copyright symbol '©'.

Editing Text

Other editing could include deleting unwanted words or adding extra text in the document. All these operations are very easy to carry out. For small deletions, such as letters or words, the easiest method is to use the <Del> or <BkSp> keys.

With the <Del> key, position the cursor on the left of the first letter you want to delete and press <Del>. With the <BkSp> key, position the cursor immediately to the right of the character to be deleted and press <BkSp>. In both cases the rest of the line moves to the left to take up the space created by the deleting process.

Word processing is usually carried out in the insert mode. Any characters typed will be inserted at the cursor location (insertion point) and the following text will be pushed to the right, and down, to make room. To insert blank lines in your text, place the cursor at the beginning of the line where the blank line is needed and press <Enter>. To remove the blank line, position the cursor on it and press <Del>.

When larger scale editing is needed you have several alternatives. You could first 'select' the text to be altered, then use the **Cut, Copy** and **Paste** operations available in the **Edit** sub-menu, or more easily, click on their Toolbar button alternatives shown here.

Another method of copying or moving text is to use the 'drag and drop' facility which requires you to highlight a word, grab it with the left mouse button depressed, and drop it in the required place in your text, as shown here to the left.

These operations will be discussed, in more detail, in the following sections of this chapter.

Selecting Text

The procedure in Word, as with most Windows based applications, is first to select the text to be altered before any operation, such as formatting or editing, can be carried out on it (use the **PC User1** file to experiment). Selected text is highlighted on the screen. This can be carried out in two main ways:

A. Using the keyboard, to select:

• A block of text.	Position the cursor on the first character to be selected and hold down the <Shift> key while using the arrow keys to highlight the required text, then release the <Shift> key.
• From the present position to the end of the line.	Use <Shift+End>.
• From the present cursor position to the beginning of the line.	Use <Shift+Home>.
• From the present cursor position to the end of the document.	Use <Shift+Ctrl+End>.
• From the present cursor position to the beginning of the document.	Use <Shift+Ctrl+Home>.
• Select the whole document.	Use <Ctrl A>

B. *With the mouse, to select:*

- A block of text.

  Press down the left mouse button at the beginning of the block and while holding it pressed, drag the cursor across the block so that the desired text is highlighted, then release the mouse button.

- A word.

  Double-click within the word.

- A line.

  Place the mouse pointer in the selection bar (just to the left of the line, when it changes to an arrow ⇗) click once. For multiple lines, drag this pointer down.

- A sentence.

  Hold the <Ctrl> key down and click in the sentence.

- A paragraph.

  Place the mouse pointer in the selection bar and double-click (for multiple paragraphs, after selecting the first paragraph, drag the pointer in the selection bar) or triple-click in the paragraph.

- The whole document.

  Place the mouse pointer in the selection bar, hold the <Ctrl> key down and click once.

With Word 2003 you can select non-contiguous text and graphics (ones that aren't next to each other), by selecting the first item you want, such as a word, sentence or paragraph, holding down the <Ctrl> key and selecting any other items from anywhere in the document. You can only select text, or graphics in this way, not both at the same time.

Copying Blocks of Text

Once text has been selected it can be copied to another location in your present document, to another Word document, or to another Windows application, via the system clipboard. As with most of the editing and formatting operations there are several alternative ways of doing this, as follows:

- Use the **Edit, Copy** command sequence from the menu, to copy the selected text to the clipboard, moving the cursor to the start of where you want the copied text to be placed, and using the **Edit, Paste** command.

- Use the quick key combinations, <Ctrl+C> (or <Ctrl+Ins>) to copy and <Ctrl+V> (or <Shift+Ins>) to paste. This does not require the menu bar to be activated.

- Use the **Copy** and **Paste** Standard Toolbar buttons; you can of course only use this method with a mouse.

To copy the same text again to another location, or to any open document window or application, move the cursor to the new location and paste it there with any of these methods.

The above operations use the system clipboard which prior to Office XP only held the last item cut or copied. Microsoft Office 2003 comes with a clipboard in which you can store 24 cut or copied items until they are needed. Each item is displayed as a thumbnail on the new **Clipboard** Task Pane as shown in Fig. 5.5 on the next page.

The Clipboard Task Pane

To illustrate how the Clipboard contents can be exploited, open the **PC User1** file (if not already opened) in Word.

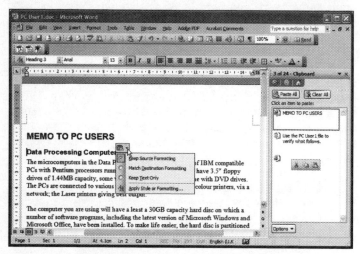

Fig. 5.5 Pasting from the Clipboard Task Pane.

Next, select the first line of the memo (in this case "MEMO TO PC USERS") and delete it using either the **Edit**, **Cut** menu command, the <Ctrl+X> key combination, or by clicking the Delete icon on the Toolbar. Now open the **Clipboard** Task Pane by selecting it from its drop-down menu (or by using the **Edit**, **Office Clipboard** command). The **Clipboard** Task Pane in Fig. 5.5, shows two text items and a picture (yours might only show the deleted line of the memo). Clicking on an item on the Clipboard, pastes that item at the cursor position within the memo.

Note the appearance of the **Smart Tag** button in Fig. 5.5 which, by default, is always placed just under newly pasted text in Word. Clicking this button, as shown above, opens a menu which lets you control the style and formatting of the pasted text. If you don't want to make any formatting changes to the text, just carry on and the smart tag will 'go away'.

Moving Blocks of Text

Selected text can be moved to any location in the same document by either of the following:

- Using the **Edit, Cut** command or <Ctrl+X> (or <Shift+Del>).

- Clicking the **Cut** Toolbar button, shown here.

Next, move the cursor to the required new location and use any of the previously described procedures to paste the text where you want it.

The moved text will be placed at the cursor location and will force any existing text to make room for it. This operation can be cancelled by simply pressing <Esc>. Once moved, multiple copies of the same text can be produced by other **Paste** operations.

Drag and Drop Operations

 Selected text, or graphics, can be **copied** by holding the <Ctrl> key depressed and dragging the mouse with the left button held down. The copy drag pointer is an arrow with two attached squares, as shown here - the vertical dotted line showing the point of insertion. The new text will insert itself where placed, even if the overstrike mode is in operation. Text copied by this method is not placed on the clipboard, so multiple copies are not possible as with other methods.

 Selected text can be **moved** by dragging the mouse with the left button held down. The move drag pointer is an arrow with an attached square - the vertical dotted line showing the point of insertion.

Deleting Blocks of Text

When text is 'cut' with the **Edit, Cut** command, or by clicking the **Cut** toolbar button, it is removed from the document, but placed on the clipboard. When the <Del> or <BkSp> keys are used, however, the text is deleted but not put on the clipboard.

The Undo Command

If you make a mistake when using the delete command, all is not lost as long as you act promptly. The **Edit, Undo** command or <Ctrl+Z> reverses your most recent editing or formatting commands.

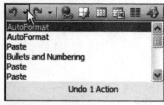

Fig. 5.6 The Undo Cascade Menu.

You can also use the **Undo** Standard Toolbar button, shown here, to undo one of several editing or formatting mistakes (press the down arrow to the right of the button to see a list of your recent changes, as shown here).

Undo does not reverse any action once editing changes have been saved to file. Only editing done since the last save can be reversed.

Finding and Changing Text

Word allows you to search for specifically selected text, or character combinations with the **Find** or the **Replace** options on the **Edit** command sub-menu.

Using the **Find** option (<Ctrl+F>), will highlight each occurrence of the supplied text in turn so that you can carry out some action on it, such as change its font or appearance. Using the **Replace** option (<Ctrl+H>), allows you to specify what replacement is to be automatically carried out. For example, in a long article you may decide to replace every occurrence of the word 'microcomputers' with the word 'PCs'.

To illustrate the **Replace** procedure, select the option from the **Edit** sub-menu (or use the quick key combination <Ctrl+H>). This opens the Find and Replace dialogue box shown on the next page with the **More** button clicked. Towards the bottom of the dialogue box, there are five check boxes; the first two can be used to match the case of letters in the search string, or a whole word, while the last three are used for wildcard, 'sounds like' or 'word forms' matching.

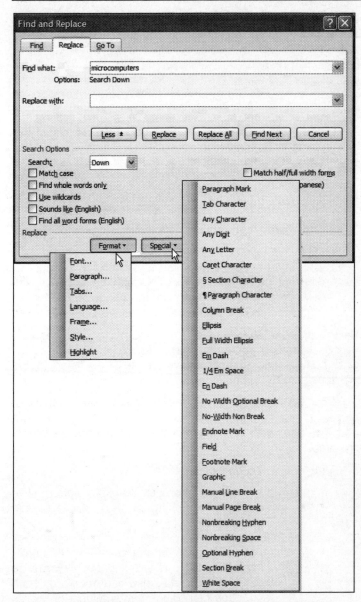

Fig. 5.7 A Composite of the Find and Replace Dialogue Box.

The two buttons, **Format** and **Special**, situated at the bottom of the dialogue box, let you control how the search is carried out. The lists of available options, when either of these buttons is pressed, are displayed in Fig. 5.7. You will of course only see one or the other, but not both as shown here. You can force both the search and the replace operations to work with exact text attributes. For example, selecting:

*   The **Font** option from the list under **Format**, displays a dialogue box in which you select a font (such as Arial, Times New Roman, etc.); a font-style (such as regular, bold, italic, etc.); an underline option (such as single, double, etc.); and special effects (such as strike-through, superscript, subscript, etc.).

*   The **Paragraph** option, lets you control indentation, spacing (before and after), and alignment.

*   The **Style** option, allows you to search for, or replace, different paragraph styles. This can be useful if you develop a new style and want to change all the text of another style in a document to use your preferred style.

Using the **Special** button, you can search for, and replace, various specified document marks, tabs, hard returns, etc., or a combination of both these and text, as listed in the previous screen dump.

Below we list only two of the many key combinations of special characters that could be typed into the **Find what** and **Replace with** boxes when the **Use wildcards** box is checked.

Type	*To find or replace*
?	Any single character within a pattern. For example, searching for nec?, will find <u>neck</u>, con<u>nect</u>, etc.
*	Any string of characters. For example, searching for c*r, will find such words as <u>cellar</u>, <u>chillier</u>, etc., also parts of words such as <u>character</u>, and combinations of words such as <u>connect, cellar</u>.

The Research Task Pane

Clicking the **Research** toolbar button, shown here, opens the new **Research** Task Pane (Fig. 5.8). This facility is available with all the Office applications and allows you to reference multiple sources of information, which could be found on your computer or the Internet, without leaving an Office program.

For example, you could look up words or phrases in the Microsoft Encarta English dictionary (if installed - see message pointed to in Fig. 5.8), which contains approximately 400,000 entries, and also includes definitions, word histories, pronunciation keys, and word usage notes. You can also add other dictionaries, which are then compared against Encarta standards to ensure you receive the best results.

Another source of information is the Thesaurus where you could look up synonyms and insert them into your document directly from the Research Task Pane.

Fig. 5.8 The Research Task Pane.

In the list of results on the Research Task Pane, you can also click related links that take you to additional information on the Internet. You can also get translations using bilingual dictionaries on your computer or online, or get stock quotes and company information while you work. The choice is yours!

Page Breaks

The program automatically inserts a 'soft' page break in a document when a page of typed text is full. To force a

manual, or hard page break, either use the <Ctrl+Enter> keystrokes, or use the **Insert**, **Break** command and select **Page break** in the dialogue box, shown in Fig. 5.9.

Pressing **OK** places a series of dots across the page to indicate the page break (this can only be seen in Normal view), as shown in Fig. 5.10 below. If you are in Print Layout view or Reading view, the second paragraph below appears

Fig. 5.9 Break Box.

on the next page. To delete manual page breaks place the cursor on the line of dots, and press the <Del> key. In Print Layout view or Reading view, place the cursor at the beginning of the second page and press the <BkSp> key.

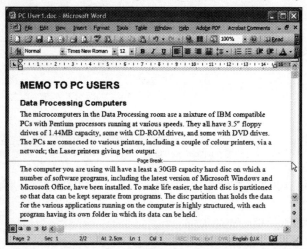

Fig. 5.10 A Hard Page Break in Normal View.

Soft page breaks which are automatically entered by the program at the end of pages, cannot be deleted.

Using the Spell Checker

The package has a very comprehensive spell checker which whenever it thinks it has found a misspelled word, underlines it with a red wavy line. To correct your document, right-click such words for alternatives, as we saw earlier.

However, the spell checker can also be used in another way. To spell check your document, either click the **Spelling and Grammar** Toolbar button, shown here, or use the **Tools**, **Spelling and Grammar** command (or **F7**) to open the dialogue box shown in Fig. 5.11 below.

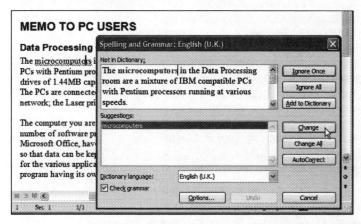

Fig. 5.11 Checking a Whole Document's Spelling.

Make sure you are using the correct dictionary by checking in the **Dictionary language** box. With us this gave an enormous list of English, French and Spanish speaking country options. If you want to check a word or paragraph only, highlight it first. Once Word has found a misspelled word, you can either correct it in the **Not in Dictionary:** box, or select a word from the **Suggestions** list.

The main dictionary cannot be edited, but you can add specialised and personal dictionaries with the facility to customise and edit them. If you choose **Add**, the specified word is added to a custom dictionary.

Using the Thesaurus

If you are not sure of the meaning of a word, or you want to use an alternative word in your document, then the thesaurus is an indispensable tool. To use the thesaurus, simply place the cursor on the word you want to look up and select the **Tools, Language, Thesaurus** command, or use the <Shift+**F7**> key combination, which opens the **Research** Task Pane. As long as the word is recognised, synonyms are listed, as shown in Fig. 5.12.

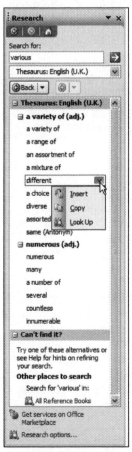

This is a very powerful tool; you can see information about an item under **a variety of (adj.)**, and under **numerous (adj.)**. Selecting a synonym displays a down-arrow against it which, when clicked, produces a drop-down menu of three items. You can choose to **Insert** the selected word in your document in place of the original word, you can **Copy** the selected word to the clipboard so it can be used later, or you can **Look Up** a synonym for this particular word.

You can use the thesaurus like a simple dictionary by typing any word into the **Search for** box and clicking the ▦ button. Again, if the word is recognised, lists of its meaning variations and synonyms will be displayed.

A quick way to get a list of alternatives to a word in your document is to right-click it and select **Synonyms** from the drop-down menu. If you select one from the list it will replace the original word. The last choice in the list activates the **Thesaurus**.

Fig. 5.12 The Thesaurus.

The Grammar Checker

We find the Grammar Checker provided with Word to be much better than that of previous versions of the package. It does not have all the pre-set styles that we are sure were never used by anyone.

To illustrate using the Grammar Checker, open the **PC User1** file (if not already opened) and at the end of it type the following sentence which we know will cause some reaction from the grammar checker.

'Use the My Computer utility which Microsoft have spent much time and effort making as intuitive as possible.'

Straight away the Grammar Checker underlines the word 'have' with a green wavy line as shown below in Fig. 5.13.

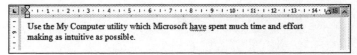

Fig. 5.13 Checking the Grammar of a Sentence.

Right-clicking the wavy line opens a shortcut menu and choosing the **Grammar** option displays the following:

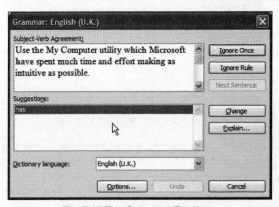

Fig. 5.14 The Grammar Checker.

The Grammar Checker has picked up what is incorrect, as expected. No other errors were flagged up in this memo. Gone are the messages about 'Passive Verb Usage' which was the obsession of the Grammar Checker in some of the older versions of Word. If you want more information on the suggested changes, try clicking the **Explain** button.

To see the Grammar Checker settings you use the **Tools, Options** command to open the Options dialogue box, and click the Spelling & Grammar tab, as shown in Fig. 5.15.

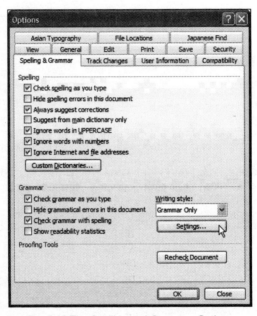

Fig. 5.15 The Spelling and Grammar Options.

As you can see, you can to a certain extent customise the way the grammar checker works. For example, clicking the **Settings** button in the above dialogue box displays the Grammar Settings dialogue box where you can make further choices.

Do spend some time with these two dialogue boxes to find out all the available options before going on.

Printing Documents

When Windows was first installed on your computer the printers you intend to use should have been selected, and the SETUP program should have installed the appropriate printer drivers. Before printing for the first time, it may be a good idea to check that your printer is in fact properly installed. To do this, click the Windows *start* button (at the left end of the Taskbar) and click the **Printers and Faxes** menu option to open the Printers folder shown in Fig. 5.16 below.

Fig. 5.16 The Windows Printers Folder.

Here, several printer drivers have been installed with the HP LaserJet 5/5M PostScript as the 'default' printer and an Acrobat Distiller 'printer' which we often use. In our case the HP LaserJet is configured to output to the printer via the parallel port LPT1 - yours may well be via a USB port. LPT1 is short for Line Printer 1 and refers to the socket at the back of your PC which is connected to your printer. Similarly, a USB port is also a socket to be found at the back of your PC.

To see how a printer is configured (whether to print to a printer port or to a file), select it by clicking its icon, then use the **File, Properties** command and click the Ports tab of the displayed dialogue box.

Next, return to or reactivate Word and, if the document you want to print is not in memory, click the **Open** Toolbar icon, then use the displayed Open dialogue box to locate and open the file, or document, you want to print, which will be found on the drive and folder on which you saved it originally.

To print your document, do one of the following:

- Click the **Print** button on the Standard Toolbar, shown here, which prints the document using the default printer and current settings.

- Use the **File**, **Print** command which opens the Print dialogue box, shown in Fig. 5.17 below.

Fig. 5.17 The Print Dialogue Box.

The settings in the Print dialogue box allow you to select the number of copies, and which pages, you want printed. You can also select to print the document, the summary information relating to that document, comments, styles, etc., in the **Print what** drop-down list.

You can even change the selected printer by clicking the down arrow against the **Name** box which displays the available printers on your system.

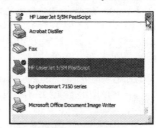

Fig. 5.18 Choosing a Different Printer.

Clicking the **Properties** button on the Print dialogue box, displays the Properties dialogue box for the selected printer which allows you to select the paper size, orientation needed, paper source, page order, etc.

The **Options** button on the Print dialogue box, gives you access to some more advanced print options, such as printing in reverse order, with or without comments, print hidden text or field codes, etc., as shown in Fig. 5.19 below.

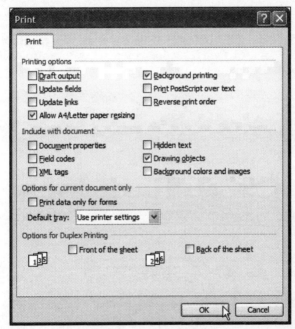

Fig. 5.19 A Printer Properties Dialogue Box.

Clicking the **OK** button on these various multilevel dialogue boxes, causes Word to accept your selections and return you to the previous level dialogue box, until the Print dialogue box is reached. Selecting **OK** on this first level dialogue box, sends print output from Word to your selection, either the printer connected to your computer, or to an encoded file on disc. Selecting **Cancel** or **Close** on any level dialogue box, aborts the selections made at that level.

Do remember that, whenever you change printers, the appearance of your document may change, as Word uses the fonts available with the newly selected printer. This can affect the line lengths, which in turn will affect both the tabulation and pagination of your document.

Print Preview

Before printing your document to paper, click the **Print Preview** button on the Standard Toolbar, or use the **File**, **Print Preview** command, to see what your print output will look like, and how much of your document will fit on your selected page size. This depends very much on the chosen font. In Fig. 5.20 below we show a preview of our example document PC Users1.doc.

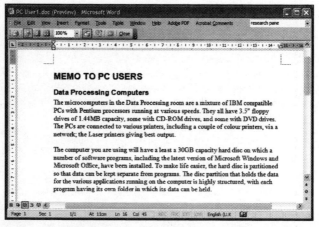

Fig. 5.20 A Print Preview of our Document.

This view allows you to see the layout of the final printed page, which could save a few trees and equally important to you, a lot of frustration and wear and tear on your printer.

The print Preview window has its own toolbar with options for magnification and number of pages actually viewed. You can even edit your document, if you want to make any last minute changes. To print the document simply click the **Print** button, or to return to your working document from a print preview display, click the **Close** button on its menu bar.

6

Formatting Word Documents

Formatting involves the appearance of individual words or even characters, the line spacing and alignment of paragraphs, and the overall page layout of the entire document. These functions are carried out in Word in several different ways.

Primary page layout is included in a document's Template and text formatting in a Template's styles. Within any document, however, you can override Paragraph Style formats by applying text formatting and enhancements manually to selected text. To immediately cancel manual formatting, select the text and use the **Edit, Undo** command, or (<Ctrl+Z>). The selected text reverts to its original format. In the long term, you can cancel manual formatting by selecting the text and using the <Shift+Ctrl+N> key stroke. The text then reverts to its style format.

Formatting Text

If you use TrueType fonts, which are automatically installed when you set up Windows, Word uses the same font to display text on the screen and to print on paper, unless you display text on screen in the **Reading Layout** mode which uses ClearType fonts instead. The TrueType screen fonts provide a very close approximation of printed characters. TrueType font names are preceded by ᵀᵣ in the Font box on the Formatting Bar.

If you use non-TrueType fonts, then use a screen font that matches your printer font. If a matching font is not available, or if your printer driver does not provide screen font information, Windows chooses the screen font that most closely resembles the printer font.

Originally, the title and subtitle of the **PC User1** memo, were selected from the default Normal style as 'Heading 1' and 'Heading 3', which were in the 16 and 13 point size Arial typeface, respectively, while the main text was typed in 12 point size Times New Roman.

To change this memo into what appears on the screen dump displayed below, first select the title of the memo and format it to italics, 18 point size Arial and centre it between the margins, then select the subtitle and format it to 14 point size Arial. Both title and subtitle are in bold as part of the definition of their respective paragraph style. Finally select both paragraphs of the main body of the memo, and format it to 12 point size Arial. Notice in each case that the Style details in the Style box on the Formatting Toolbar are changed to show the manual formatting that was added. This shows as 'Normal + Arial' in Fig. 6.1 below.

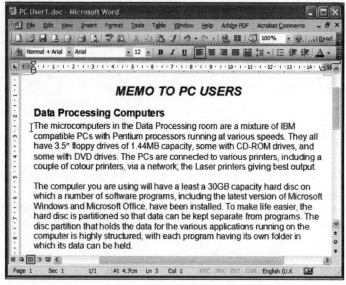

Fig. 6.1 The Reformatted PC Users Memo.

All of this formatting can be achieved by using the buttons on the Formatting Bar (see also the section entitled 'Paragraph Alignment'). Save the result under the new filename **PC User2**, using the **File, Save As** command.

Text Enhancements

In Word all manual formatting, including the selection of font, point size, style (bold, italic, highlight, strike-through, hidden and capitals), colour, super/subscript, spacing and various underlines, are carried out by first selecting the text and then executing the formatting command.

With some actions the easiest way of activating the formatting commands is from the Formatting Bar. With others you have to use the **Format**, **Font** menu command, and select options from the dialogue box below.

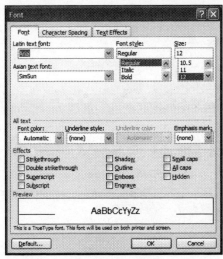

Fig. 6.2 The Font Box.

Yet another method is by using quick keys, some of which are listed below:

To Format	*Type*
Bold	Ctrl+B
Italic	Ctrl+I
Underline	Ctrl+U
Word underline	Ctrl+Shift+W

There are quick keys to do almost anything, but the ones listed here are the most useful and the easiest to remember.

Paragraph Alignment

Word defines a paragraph, as any text which is followed by a paragraph mark, which is created by pressing the <Enter> key. So single line titles, as well as sections of long typed text, can form paragraphs.

 The paragraph symbol, shown here, is only visible in your text if you have selected **Show/Hide** ¶ button from the Standard Toolbar, or used <Ctrl+*>.

Word allows you to align a paragraph at the left margin (the default), at the right margin, centred between both margins, or justified between both margins. As with most operations there are several ways to perform alignment in Word. Three such methods are:

- Using buttons on the **Formatting Bar**.
- Using keyboard short cuts.
- Using the **Format**, **Paragraph** menu command.

The table below describes some useful buttons on the Formatting Bar and their keystroke shortcuts.

Buttons on Formatting Bar	Paragraph Alignment	Keystrokes
	Left	<Ctrl+L>
	Centred	<Ctrl+E>
	Right	<Ctrl+R>
	Justified	<Ctrl+J>
	Distributed	<Ctrl+Shift+J>

Paragraph Spacing

Using the **Format**, **Paragraph** command displays the Paragraph dialogue box, as shown in Fig. 6.3 with its **Indents and Spacing** tab selected.

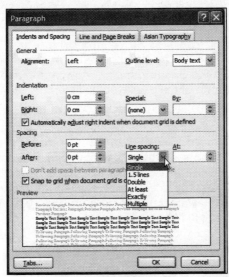

Fig. 6.3 The Paragraph Box.

The settings in this box will affect the current paragraph (with the insertion point in it), or any selected paragraphs. Here you can specify any **Left, Right**, or **Special** indentation required, and set your paragraph line spacing to single-line, 1.5 line, or double-line spacing. You can even set the spacing to any value you want by using the **At Least** option, as shown above, then specify what interval you want.

The available shortcut keys for paragraph spacing are as follows:

To Format	Type
Single-spaced lines	Ctrl+1
One-and-a-half-spaced lines	Ctrl+5
Double-spaced lines	Ctrl+2

Whichever of the above methods is used, formatting can take place either before or after the text is entered. If formatting is selected first, then text will type in the chosen format until a further formatting command is given. If, on the other hand, you choose to enter text and then format it afterwards, you must first select the text to be formatted, then activate the formatting.

Line spacing can also be controlled from the Formatting Toolbar by clicking the down arrow against the **Line Spacing** button shown here, and selecting one of the displayed options.

Word gives you the choice of 5 units to work with, inches, centimetres, millimetres, points or picas. These can be selected by using the **Tools**, **Options** command, choosing the **General** tab of the displayed Options dialogue box, and clicking the down arrow against the **Measurement units** list box, shown open here in Fig. 6.4. We have selected to work in the default centimetres.

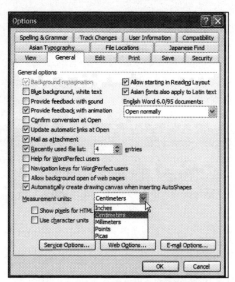

Fig. 6.4 Setting Measurement Units.

Indenting Text

Most documents will require some form of paragraph indenting. An indent is the space between the margin and the edge of the text in the paragraph. When an indent is set (on the left or right side of the page), any justification on that side of the page sets at the indent, not the page margin.

To illustrate indentation, open the file **PC User2**, select the first paragraph, and then choose the **Format**, **Paragraph** command. In the **Indentation** field, select 2.5 cm for both **Left** and **Right**, as shown in Fig. 6.5 below. On clicking **OK**, the first selected paragraph is displayed indented. Our screen dump shows the result of the indentation as well as the settings on the Paragraph dialogue box which caused it.

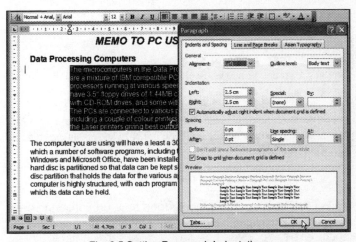

Fig. 6.5 Setting Paragraph Indentation.

You can also use the Formatting Bar buttons, shown below, to decrease or increase the indent of selected text.

 Use this button to decrease indent.

 Use this button to increase indent.

The **Indentation** option in the Paragraph dialogue box, can be used to create 'hanging' indents, where all the lines in a paragraph, including any text on the first line that follows a tab, are indented by a specified amount. This is often used in lists to emphasise certain points.

To illustrate the method, use the **PC User1** file and add at the end of it the text shown below. After you have typed the text in, save the enlarged memo as **PC User3**, before going on with formatting the new text.

In Windows you can work with files in three different ways:

Name Description

My Computer Use the My Computer utility from the Start menu, which Microsoft has spent much time and effort making as intuitive as possible.

Explorer Use the Windows Explorer from the Start, All Programs, Accessories sub-menu.

MS-DOS Use the Command Prompt window from the Start, All Programs, Accessories sub-menu, if you prefer to and are an expert with the DOS commands.

Fig. 6.6 Additional Text to be Typed in Word.

Saving the work at this stage is done as a precaution in case anything goes wrong with the formatting - it is sometimes much easier to reload a saved file, than it is to try to unscramble a wrongly formatted document!

Next, highlight the last four paragraphs above, use the **Format**, **Paragraph** command, and select 'Hanging' under **Special** and 3 cm under **By**. On clicking the **OK** button, the text formats as shown in the composite screen dump of Fig. 6.7, but it is still highlighted. To remove the highlighting, click the mouse button anywhere on the page. The second and following lines of the selected paragraphs, should be indented 3 cm from the left margin.

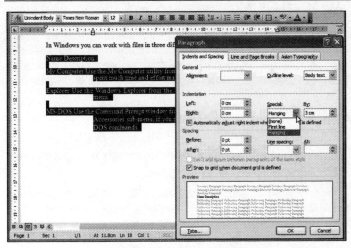

Fig. 6.7 Setting Hanging Indents Manually

This is still not very inspiring, so to complete the effect we will edit the first lines of each paragraph as follows:

Place the cursor in front of the word 'Description' and press the <Tab> key once. This places the start of the word in the same column as the indented text of the other paragraphs. To complete the effect place tabs before the words 'Use' in the next three paragraphs, until your hanging indents are correct, as shown in Fig. 6.8 below.

In Windows you can work with files in three different ways:	
Name	Description
My Computer	Use the My Computer utility from the Start menu, which Microsoft has spent much time and effort making as intuitive as possible.
Explorer	Use the Windows Explorer from the Start, All Programs, Accessories sub-menu.
MS-DOS	Use the Command Prompt window from the Start, All Programs, Accessories sub-menu, if you prefer to and are an expert with the DOS commands.

Fig. 6.8 Text Formatted with Hanging Indents.

This may seem like a complicated rigmarole to go through each time you want the hanging indent effect, but with Word you will eventually set up all your indents, etc., as styles in templates. Then all you do is click in a paragraph to produce them. We will discuss this towards the end of this chapter.

Adding a Drop Capital

Another text feature that you may want to use at times is to make the first letter of a paragraph a large dropped initial capital letter, as shown here.

With Word that is ridiculously easy. Just place the insertion point at the beginning of the existing paragraph and action the **Format**, **Drop Cap** menu command. This opens the Drop Cap dialogue box, shown in our composite Fig. 6.9. As is often the case, this gives the settings needed to produce the result shown. You would not normally see them both together.

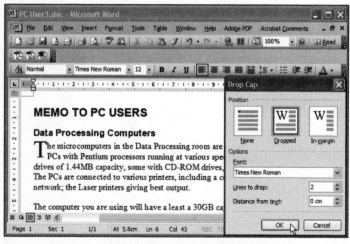

Fig. 6.9 Setting a Dropped Capital Letter.

You can choose between **Dropped** and **In margin** for the position of the initial capital letter, change the **Font** (as we have done) and select how many **Lines to drop**.

The new first letter is actually a graphic image now. To remove the effect if you decide you don't want it, select the image by clicking it, open the dialogue box with the **Format**, **Drop Cap** command and select **None**.

When you finish formatting the document, save it under its current filename either with the **File, Save** command (<Ctrl+S>), or by clicking the **Save** button. This command does not display a dialogue box, so you use it when you do not need to make any changes during the saving operation.

Inserting Bullets

Bullets are small characters you can insert, anywhere you like, in the text of your document to improve visual impact. In Word there are several choices for displaying lists with bullets or numbers. As well as the two Formatting Bar buttons, others are made available through the **Format, Bullets and Numbering** command, which displays the dialogue box in Fig. 6.10.

Fig. 6.10 Setting Bullets and Numbering Styles.

You can select any of the bullets shown here, or you could click the **Customize** button to change the shape, font and size of the bullet, choose a character, and set the indentation in the Customize Bulleted List box shown on the left in Fig. 6.11.

Fig. 6.11 Choosing Custom Bullet Pictures.

Further, by pressing the **Picture** button on the Customized Bulleted List dialogue box you can select from an enormous number of bullet pictures, as shown on the right of Fig. 6.11. If none of these images suit, you can even **Import** a graphic image yourself to use as bullets. Very comprehensive.

If you select the **Numbered** or **Outline Numbered** tabs, shown in Fig. 6.10, similar dialogue boxes are displayed, giving you a choice of several numbering or outline (multilevel) systems.

Once inserted, you can copy, move or cut a bulleted paragraph in the same way as any other text. However, you can not delete a bullet with the <BkSp> or <Del> keys. To do this, you need to place the insertion point in the line and click the **Bullets** Toolbar button, shown here. Once you have set up a customised bullet, clicking this button in a paragraph will use it.

Inserting Date and Time

You can insert today's date, the date the current document was created or was last revised, or a date or time that reflects the current system date and time into a document. Therefore, the date can be a date that changes, or a date that always stays the same. In either case, the date is inserted in a date field.

To insert a date field in your document, place the cursor where you want to insert the date, select the **Insert**, **Date and Time** command and choose one of the displayed date formats which suits you from the dialogue box shown in Fig. 6.12 below which is a composite of the operation required and the result of that operation.

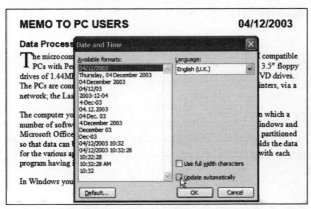

Fig. 6.12 Inserting Dates and Times in a Document.

If you save a document with a date field in it and you open it a few days later, the date shown on it will be the original date the document was created. Most of the time this will probably be what you want, but should you want the displayed date to always update to the current date whenever the document is opened, check the **Update automatically** box, pointed to in Fig. 6.12, and then click the **OK** button.

Note that many of Word's dialogue boxes have a **Default** button on them, as above. If you click this button you will make the settings active in the box at the time, the default ones in future documents opened with the Normal template.

Comments and Tracked Changes

Another powerful feature of Word is the facility to add comments and to track changes made to a document. Comments are notes, or annotations, that an author or reviewer adds to a document and in Word 2003 they are displayed in balloons in the margin of the document or in the Reviewing Pane, as shown in Fig. 6.13. A tracked change is a mark that shows where a deletion, insertion, or other editing change has been made in a document.

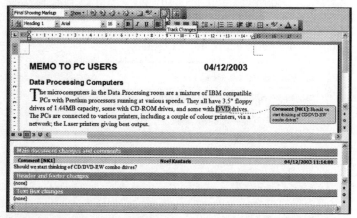

Fig. 6.13 A Comment in a Document with the Reviewing Pane Open.

To quickly display or hide tracked changes or comments (known as mark-up) use the **View**, **Markup** menu command. To add a comment, place the pointer in the correct location, use the **Insert**, **Comment** command, and type the comment into the pane that opens at the bottom of the screen. If the Reviewing toolbar shown above is hidden, simply right-click any toolbar, and then click Reviewing on the shortcut menu. To open the reviewing pane, as shown above, use the **Show**, **Reviewing Pane** command from the Reviewing toolbar.

You can print a document with mark-up to keep a record of any changes made. If you want to see comments and tracked changes in balloons you must be in Print Layout, Web Layout, or Reading Layout view.

Formatting with Page Tabs

You can format text in columns by using tab stops. Word has default left tab stops at 1.27 cm intervals. By default the symbol for a left tab appears in the tab type button at the left edge of the ruler as shown in Fig 6.14 below.

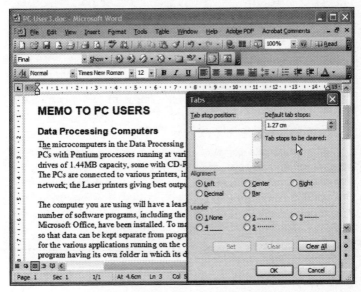

Fig. 6.14 The Ruler and Tabs Dialogue Box.

To set tabs, use either the **Format**, **Tabs** command which opens the Tabs dialogue box shown above, or click on the tab type button (which cycles through the available tab stops) until the type you want is showing and then click the required position on the lower half of the ruler. To remove an added tab, just drag it off the ruler.

To clear the ruler of tab settings press the **Clear All** button in the Tabs dialogue box. When you set a tab stop on the ruler, all default tab stops to the left of the one you are setting are removed. Tab stops apply either to the paragraph containing the cursor, or to any selected paragraphs.

The tab stop types available have the following functions:

Button	Name	Effect
L	**Left**	Left aligns text after the tab stop.
⊥	**Centre**	Centres text on tab stop.
⌐	**Right**	Right aligns text at the tab stop.
⊥	**Decimal**	Aligns decimal point with tab stop.
I	**Bar**	Inserts a vertical line at the tab stop.

The tab type button actually cycles through two more types, first line indent and hanging indent. This gives you a quick way of adding these indents to the ruler.

If you want tabular text to be separated by characters instead of by spaces, select one of the four available characters from the **Leader** box in the Tabs dialogue box. The options are none (the default), dotted, dashed, underline, or embolden dotted. The Contents pages of this book are set with right tabs and dotted leader characters.

Having made a choice and specified the **Tab stop position** required, click the **Set** button before clicking **OK**. Now using the Tab key displays the selected leader characters. If you don't like what you see, press the **Clear All** button in the Tabs dialogue box. This will take you back to the default Tab settings.

Note: As all paragraph formatting, such as tab stops, is placed at the end of a paragraph, if you want to carry the formatting of the current paragraph to the next, press <Enter>. If you don't want formatting to carry on, press the down arrow key instead.

Formatting with Styles

We saw earlier on page 82, how you can format your work using Paragraph Styles, but we confined ourselves to using the default **Normal** styles only. In this section we will get to grips with how to create, modify, use, and manage styles.

As mentioned previously, a Paragraph Style is a set of formatting instructions which you save so that you can use it repeatedly within a document or in different documents. A collection of Paragraph Styles can be placed in a Template which could be appropriate for, say, all your memos, so it can be used to preserve uniformity. It maintains consistency and saves time by not having to format each paragraph individually.

Further, should you decide to change a style, all the paragraphs associated with that style reformat automatically. Finally, if you want to provide a pattern for shaping a final document, then you use what is known as a Template. All documents which have not been assigned a document template, use the **Normal.dot** global template, by default.

Paragraph Styles

Paragraph Styles contain paragraph and character formats and a name can be attached to these formatting instructions. From then on, applying the style name is the same as formatting that paragraph with the same instructions.

With Word you create your styles by example using the **Styles and Formatting** Task Pane, as we show in Fig. 6.15 on the next page.

Creating a New Paragraph Style: Previously, we spent some time manually creating some hanging indents in the last few paragraphs of the **PC User3** document. Open that document and display the **Styles and Formatting** Task Pane (see Fig. 6.15) by clicking its toolbar button, shown here. Place the insertion pointer in one of the previously created hanging indent paragraphs, say, in the 'Name Description' line.

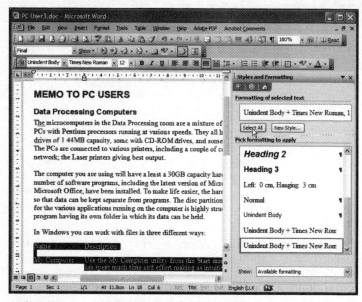

Fig. 6.15 Creating a New Style.

Notice that the selected item in the **Pick formatting to apply** list in the Task Pane has a rectangular selection marker around it. This in fact represents an unnamed style with the formatting we used to create the hanging indents. If you click the **Select All** button in the Task Pane all of our paragraphs with this formatting are highlighted in the main document.

Next, click the **New Style** button in the Task Pane to open the New Style box shown in Fig. 6.16.

Fig. 6.16 The New Style Box.

Now type the new style name you want to create in the **Name** text box, say, 'Hanging Indent', then select the **Add to template** option at the bottom of the box, and click **OK** to accept your changes.

Finally, one by one, highlight the other three paragraphs with hanging indents and change their style to the new 'Hanging Indent', by selecting the new style either from the list in the **Styles and Formatting** Task Pane, or from the drop-down list displayed when the **Style** button on the Formatting Toolbar is used.

We can now delete the redundant style on which we based our new Hanging Indent style. To do so, right-click in turn the two entries in the **Pick formatting to apply** list, and select **Delete** from the drop-down menu, as shown in Fig. 6.17 below. Save the result as **PC User4**, make yourself a drink, and relax - you have earned it!

Fig. 6.17 Our New Style in Action.

You could also have a look at Word's built-in styles by using the **Format, Theme** menu command and clicking the **Style Gallery** button on the displayed Theme dialogue box. There are over thirty available styles, one of which might suit your type of document. Try them with the **PC User4** file open, as it reformats your document on a viewing pane. Some of them may need installing though, but it will carry this out for you without too much trouble.

Document Templates

A document template provides the overall pattern of your final document. It can contain:

- Styles to control your paragraph and formats.

- Page set-up options.

- Boilerplate text, which is text that remains the same in every document.

- AutoText, which is standard text and graphics that you could insert in a document by typing the name of the AutoText entry.

- Macros, which are programs that can change the menus and key assignments to comply with the type of document you are creating.

- Customised shortcuts, toolbars and menus.

If you don't assign a template to a document, then the default **Normal.dot** template is used by Word. To create a new document template, you either modify an existing one, create one from scratch, or create one based on the formatting of an existing document.

Creating a Document Template

To illustrate the last point above, we will create a simple document template, which we will call **PC User**, based on the formatting of the **PC User4** document. But first, make sure you have defined the 'Hanging Indent' style as explained earlier.

To create a template based on an existing document do the following:

- Open the existing document.

- Select the **File, Save As** command which displays the Save As dialogue box, shown in Fig. 6.18.

- In the **Save as type** box, select Document Template.

Fig. 6.18 Saving a Document as a Template.

- In the **Save in** box, use the Templates folder which should have opened for you.

- In the **File name** box, type the name of the new template (PC User in our example).

- Press the **Save** button, which opens the template file **PC User.dot** in the Word working area.

- Add the text and graphics you want to appear in all new documents that you base on this template, and *delete* any items (including text) you do not want to appear.
  In our example, we deleted everything in the document, bar the heading, and added the words 'PC User Group' using **Insert, Picture, WordArt**, to obtain:

Fig. 6.19 Artwork and Text in our New Template.

- Click the **Save** button on the Toolbar, and close the document.

To use the new template, do the following:

- Use the **File**, **New** command which opens the **New Document** Task Pane. Select **General Templates** from the **New from template** section of the pane. The General tabbed sheet of the Templates box is opened, as shown in Fig. 6.20 below.

Fig. 6.20 The General Templates Including Our New One.

- Select the name of the template you want to use from the displayed list. This would be PCUser.dot in our case.

- Make sure that the radio button **Document** is selected, and click the **OK** button.

The new document will be using the selected template.
Templates can also contain Macros as well as AutoText; macros allow you to automate Word keystroke actions only, while AutoText speeds up the addition of boilerplate text and graphics into your document. However, the design of these features is beyond the scope of this book.

Don't forget that Word has a series of built-in templates to suit 'every occasion' as we touched on in page 98.

The Default Character Format

As we have seen, for all new documents Word uses the Times New Roman type font with a 12 points size as the default for the Normal style, which is contained in the Normal template. If the majority of your work demands some different font style or size, then you can change these defaults.

To change the default character formatting, use the **Format**, **Font** command, select the new defaults you want to use, and press the **Default** button, as shown in Fig. 6.21.

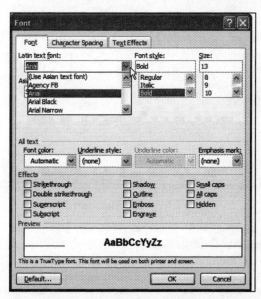

Fig. 6.21 Setting a New Default Font.

A warning box opens to make sure you really know what you are about to do. Pressing the **Yes** button, changes the default character settings for this and all subsequent new documents using the Normal template, but does not change already existing ones. Pressing **No** aborts the operation.

Special Characters and Symbols

Word 2003 has a Symbol dialogue box from which you can select characters and symbols and insert them into your document using the **Insert, Symbol** command. This is shown in Fig. 6.22 below.

Fig. 6.22 The Symbol Dialogue Box.

You should be able to find just about any symbol you require in the (Symbol) font displayed. But if not, pressing the down-arrow button next to the **Font** box, will reveal the other available character sets, as shown below in Fig. 6.23. The character sets from Webdings downwards are worth investigating as they hold a wealth of useful symbols. If you

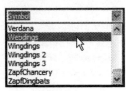

double-click the left mouse button on a character, it transfers it to your document at the insertion point.

The **AutoCorrect** button opens the box shown in Fig. 5.4 (page 101) so that you can insert any of the symbols in the **Replace text as you type** section.

Fig. 6.23 Useful Sets of Symbols.

Inserting Other Special Characters

You can include other special characters in a document, such as optional hyphens, which remain invisible until they are needed to hyphenate a word at the end of a line; non-breaking hyphens, which prevent unwanted hyphenation; non-breaking spaces, which prevent two words from splitting at the end of a line; or opening and closing single quotes.

There are two ways to insert these special characters in your document. One is to click the **Special Characters** tab of the Symbol dialogue box which reveals a long list of these special characters, as shown in Fig. 6.24. You then select one of them and click the **Insert** button.

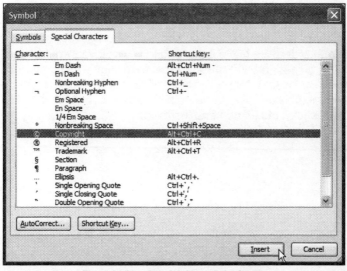

Fig. 6.24 The Special Characters Sheet.

The other way is to use the shortcut key combinations listed in Fig. 6.24, which does not require you to open the dialogue box. But you do have to remember them though!

* * *

Word has many more features, far too numerous to mention in the space allocated to this book, although we will be discussing later on how you can use Word to share information with other Microsoft applications and how to use mail merge techniques. What we have tried to do so far, is give you enough basic information so that you can have the confidence to forge ahead and explore the rest of Word's capabilities by yourself.

Perhaps, you might consider exploring page numbering, headers and footers, tables, frames, drawing, and outlining, in that order. We leave it to you. However, if you would prefer to be guided through these topics, then may we suggest you keep a lookout for our forthcoming book *Microsoft Word 2003 explained*, also to be published by BERNARD BABANI (publishing) Ltd., if demand justifies.

* * *

7

The Excel 2003 Spreadsheet

Microsoft Excel is a powerful and versatile software package which, over the years, has proved its usefulness, not only in the business world, but with scientific and engineering users as well.

The program's power lies in its ability to emulate everything that can be done using pencil, paper and a calculator. Thus, it is an 'electronic spreadsheet' or simply a 'spreadsheet', a name which is also used to describe it and other similar products. Its power is derived from the power of the computer it is running on, and the flexibility and accuracy with which it can deal with the solution of the various applications it is programmed to manage. These can vary from budgeting and forecasting to the solution of complex scientific and engineering problems.

Excel 2003 has been designed to present the new look also found in the other Office 2003 applications, and includes several improvements over previous versions. These are:

- Adoption of the Research Task Pane which we first discussed in Chapter 1, page 17.

- Adoption of XML, and features relating to document collaboration, similar to those of Word.

- Adoption of Smart Tags whose actions can now apply to individual cells. The presence of a smart tag in Excel 2003 is indicated by the placement of a small purple arrow in the bottom right-hand corner of a cell. Hovering the cursor over this, causes a drop-down menu to display.

- Adoption of an easy way of creating Lists, enhanced statistics, and support for Tablet PCs with the appearance of handwriting recognition.

Starting the Excel Program

Excel is started in Windows either by clicking the *start* button then selecting **All Programs**, **Microsoft Office**, and clicking on the Microsoft Excel icon on the cascade menu, or by double-clicking on an Excel workbook file. In the latter case the workbook will be loaded into Excel at the same time.

When you first start Excel 2003 the program momentarily displays its opening screen, shown in Fig. 7.1, and then displays the first sheet of a new workbook (more about this shortly).

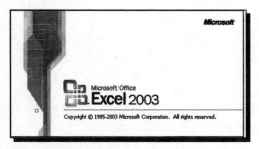

Fig. 7.1 Excel's Opening Screen.

Whether you have used a previous version of Excel or not, the first time you use the program, it might be a good idea to click the **Microsoft Excel Help** button on the Toolbar, shown here, then click the **Table of Contents** link (pointed to) in the **Excel Help** Pane part of which is shown in Fig. 7.2 below.

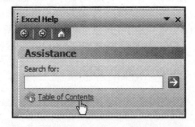

Fig. 7.2 The Table of Contents Link.

This displays the Help screen shown in Fig. 7.3. Start by clicking the **Startup and Settings** book link, then look at the **'What's new in Microsoft Office Excel 2003'** option, from which you can find out differences between this version of Excel and previous versions of the program. As you click each hypertext link, Excel displays several topics on the subject. After looking at these options, have a look at the other options displayed in the Help screen. We suggest you spend a little time here browsing through the various topics before going on.

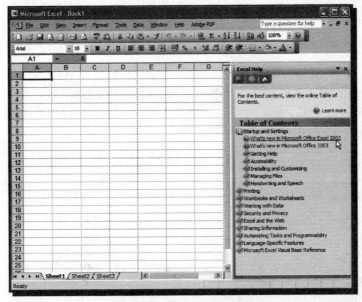

Fig. 7.3 The Microsoft Excel Help Screen.

For additional Help topics, click the **Learn more** link in the above screen, which displays in a separate window a list of additional topics, such as the 'Benefits of working with an Internet connection', 'Content that is only available online', 'Finding templates on your computer', etc. When each of these links is clicked, more information relevant to the selected topic is displayed in the window.

The Excel Screen

When Excel is loaded, a 'blank' spreadsheet screen displays with a similar Title bar, Menu bar, Toolbar and Formatting bar to those of Word. Obviously there are some differences, since the two programs serve different purposes.

The opening screen of Excel is shown in Fig. 7.4. Do note the similarities with the opening Word screen. Excel follows the usual Microsoft Windows conventions with which you should be very familiar by now. Again, for clarity we show the Formatting bar below the Standard toolbar - please refer to page 75 where we explain how this can be achieved.

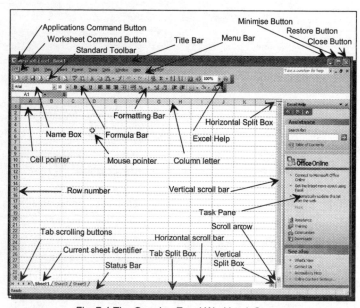

Fig. 7.4 The Opening Excel Workbook Screen.

The window as shown above takes up the full screen area. If you click on the application restore button, the top one of the two restore buttons at the top right of the screen, you can make Excel show in a smaller window. This can be useful when you are running several applications at the same time and you want to transfer between them with the mouse.

Note that the Excel window, which in this case displays an empty and untitled book (Book1), has some areas which have identical functions to those of Word (please refer to page 74), and other areas which have different functions. Below, we describe only the areas that are exclusive to Excel.

Area	*Function*
Name box	Identifies the selected cell (by name or by cell co-ordinates), chart item, or drawing object.
Formula Bar	Can display a number, a label, or the formula behind a result.
Cell pointer	Marks the current cell.
Column letter	The letter that identifies each column.
Row number	The number that identifies each row.
Tab scrolling	Clicking on these buttons, scrolls sheet tabs right or left, when there are more tabs than can be displayed at once.
Current sheet	Shows the current sheet amongst a number of sheets in a file. These are named Sheet1, Sheet2, Sheet3, and so on, by default, but can be changed to, say, North, South, East, and West. Clicking on a sheet tab, moves you to that sheet.
Tab split box	The split box which you drag left to see more of the scroll bar, or right to see more tabs.

Finally, note the location of the horizontal and vertical split boxes. The first is located at the extreme right of the screen above the 'top vertical scroll arrow' button. The second is located at the extreme bottom-right corner of the screen, to the left of the 'right horizontal scroll arrow' button. Both of these split the screen and their use will be discussed later.

Workbook Navigation

When you first enter Excel, the program sets up a series of huge electronic pages, or worksheets, in your computer's memory, many times larger than the small part shown on the screen. Individual cells are identified by column and row location (in that order), with present size extending to 256 columns and 65,536 rows. The columns are labelled from A to Z, followed by AA to AZ, BA to BZ, and so on, to IV, while the rows are numbered from 1 to 65,536.

A worksheet can be thought of as a two-dimensional table made up of rows and columns. The point where a row and column intersect is called a cell, while the reference points of a cell are known as the cell address. The active cell (A1 when you first enter the program) is boxed.

Navigation around the worksheet is achieved by using one of the following keys or key combinations:

- Pressing one of the four arrow keys ($\rightarrow\downarrow\leftarrow\uparrow$) moves the active cell one position right, down, left or up, respectively.

- Pressing the <PgDn> or <PgUp> keys moves the active cell down or up one visible page.

- Pressing the <Ctrl+$\rightarrow$> or <Ctrl+$\downarrow$> key combinations moves the active cell to the extreme right of the worksheet (column IV) or extreme bottom of the worksheet (row 65,536).

- Pressing the <Home> key, moves the active cell to the beginning of a row.

- Pressing the <Ctrl+Home> key combination moves the active cell to the home position, A1.

- Pressing the <Ctrl+End> key combination moves the active cell to the lower right corner of the worksheet's currently used area.

- Pressing the **F5** function key will display the Go To dialogue box shown in Fig. 7.5 on the next page.

In the **Go to** box a list of named ranges in the active worksheet (to be discussed shortly) is displayed, or one of the last four references from which you chose the **Go To** command.

In the **Reference** box you type the cell reference or a named range you want to move to.

Fig. 7.5 The Go To Dialogue Box.

To move the active cell with a mouse, do the following:

- Point to the cell you want to move to and click the left mouse button. If the cell is not visible, move the window by clicking on the scroll bar arrowhead that points in the direction you want to move,

- To move a page at a time, click in the scroll bar itself.

- For larger moves, drag the box in the scroll bar, but the distances moved will depend on the size of the worksheet.

When you have finished navigating around the worksheet, press the <Ctrl+Home> key combination which will move the active cell to the A1 position (provided you have not fixed titles in any rows or columns or have no hidden rows or columns - more about these later).

Note that the area within which you can move the active cell is referred to as the working area of the worksheet, while the letters and numbers in the border at the top and left of the working area give the 'co-ordinates' of the cells in a worksheet. The location of the active cell is constantly monitored by the 'selection indicator' which is to be found on the extreme left below the lower Toolbar of the application window. As the active cell is moved, this indicator displays its address, as shown in Fig. 7.6 on the next page.

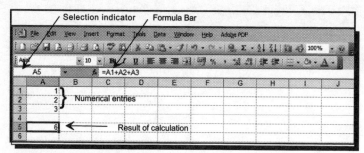

Fig. 7.6 The Selection Indicator and Formula Bar.

The contents of a cell are displayed above the column letters within what is known as the 'Formula Bar'. If you type text in the active cell, what you type appears in both the Formula Bar and the cell itself.

Typing a formula which is preceded by the equals sign (=) to, say, add the contents of three cells, causes the actual formula to appear in the Formula Bar, while the result of the actual calculation appears in the active cell when the <Enter> key is pressed.

Moving Between Sheets

You can scroll between sheets by clicking one of the arrows situated to the left of Sheet1, as shown below. We have labelled these as 'Tab scrolling buttons'. The inner arrows scroll sheets one at a time in the direction of the arrow, while the outer arrows scroll to the end, or beginning, of the group of available sheets. A sheet is then made current by clicking its tab.

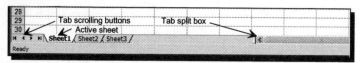

Fig. 7.7 The Active Sheet and Tab Scrolling Buttons.

With the keyboard, you can scroll one sheet at a time, and make it active at the same time, by using the <Ctrl+PgDn> key combination. Using <Ctrl+PgUp> scrolls in the reverse direction.

To display more sheet tabs at a time, drag the split box to the right. The reverse action displays less sheet tabs. To rename sheets, double-click at their tab, then type a new name to replace the highlighted name of the particular sheet tab.

To insert a sheet in front of a certain sheet, make that sheet current, then use the **Insert, Worksheet** menu command sequence. To delete a sheet, make it current and use the **Edit, Delete Sheet** command.

Rearranging Sheet Order

If you need to rearrange the order in which sheets are being held in a workbook, you can do so by dragging a particular sheet to its new position, as shown in Fig. 7.8.

Fig. 7.8 Moving an Active Sheet.

While you are dragging the tab of the sheet you want to move, the mouse pointer changes to an arrow pointing to a sheet. The small solid arrowhead to the left of the mouse pointer indicates the place where the sheet you are moving will be placed.

Grouping Worksheets

You can select several sheets to group them together so that data entry, editing, or formatting can be made easier and more consistent.

To select adjacent sheets, click the first sheet tab, hold down the <Shift> key and then click the last sheet tab in the group. To select non-adjacent sheets, click the first sheet tab, hold down the <Ctrl> key and then click the other sheet tabs you want to group together.

Selecting sheets in the above manner, causes the word '[Group]' to appear in the Title bar of the active window, and the tabs of the selected sheets to be shown in white. To cancel the selection, click at the tab of any sheet which is not part of the selected group.

Selecting a Range of Cells

To select a range of cells, say, A3:C3, point to cell A3, then:

- Press the left mouse button, and while holding it pressed, drag the mouse to the right.

Fig. 7.9 Selecting a Range of Cells.

To select a range from the keyboard, first make active the first cell in the range, then:

- Hold down the <Shift> key and use the right arrow key (→) to highlight the required range.

To select a 3D range, across several sheets, select the range in the first sheet, then:

- Release the mouse button, hold down the <Shift> key, and click the Tab of the last sheet in the range.

Shortcut Menus

While a range of cells in a sheet is selected, or a group of sheets is active, you can access a shortcut menu of relevant commands by pressing the right mouse button. This produces a shortcut menu, shown in Fig. 7.10, of the most common commands relevant to what you are doing at the time.

Fig. 7.10 A Shortcut Menu.

Viewing Multiple Workbook Sheets

To see more clearly what you are doing when working with multiple workbook sheets, use the **Insert, Worksheet** command to add a fourth sheet to your Workbook. Then use the **Window, New Window** command to add three extra windows to your worksheet. Next, type the text '1st' in location A1 of Sheet1 of window 1, the text '2nd' in location A1 of Sheet2 of window 2, and so on. Finally, use the **Window, Arrange, Tiled** command to display the four sheets as shown in Fig. 7.11. What we have done below is to make active Sheet1 in Book1:1, Sheet2 in Book1:2, and so on, to demonstrate that each window contains all four sheets.

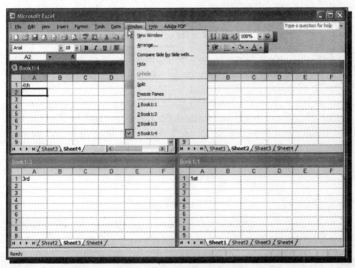

Fig. 7.11 Multiple Workbook Sheets in Tile View.

To move from one window to another, simply point with the mouse to the cell of the window you want to go to and click the left mouse button. To display a different sheet in each window, go to a window and click the sheet's tab.

To return to single-window view mode from a tiled or cascade mode, click the maximise button of the active window.

Entering Information

We will now investigate how information can be entered into a worksheet. But first, make sure you are in Sheet1, then return to the Home (A1) position, by pressing the <Ctrl+Home> key combination, then type the words:

    Project Analysis

As you type, the characters appear in both the 'Formula Bar' and the active cell. If you make a mistake, press the <BkSp> key to erase the previous letter or the <Esc> key to start again. When you have finished, press <Enter>.

Note that what you have just typed in has been entered in cell A1, even though the whole of the word ANALYSIS appears to be in cell B1. If you use the right arrow key to move the active cell to B1 you will see that the cell is indeed empty.

Typing any letter at the beginning of an entry into a cell results in a 'text' entry being formed automatically, otherwise known as a 'label'. If the length of the text is longer than the width of a cell, it will continue into the next cell to the right of the current active cell, provided that cell is empty, otherwise the displayed information will be truncated.

To edit information already in a cell, either

* double-click the cell in question, or

* make that cell the active cell and press the **F2** function key.

The cursor keys, the <Home> and <End> keys, as well as the <Ins> and <Del> keys can be used to move the cursor and/or edit information as required.

You can also 'undo' the last 16 actions carried out since the program was last in the **Ready** mode, by either using the **Edit, Undo Entry** command (<Ctrl+Z>), or clicking the **Undo** button.

Next, move the active cell to B3 and type

    Jan

Pressing the right arrow key (→) will automatically enter the typed information into the cell and also move the active cell one cell to the right, in this case to C3. Now type

    Feb

and press <Enter>.

The looks of a worksheet can be enhanced somewhat by using different types of borders around specific cells. To do

this, first select the range of cells, then click at the down arrow of the **Borders** button on the Formatting Toolbar, shown here, which displays twelve different types of borders (Fig. 7.12). In our example, we have selected the cell range A3:C3, then we chose the 8th border from the display table.

Fig. 7.12 Adding Borders to a Cell Range.

Next, move to cell A4 and type the label **Income**, then enter the numbers **14000** and **15000** in cells B4 and C4, respectively, as shown below, but note that by default the labels **Jan** and **Feb** are left justified, while the numbers are right justified.

Fig. 7.13 Default Justification of Labels and Numbers.

Changing Text Alignment and Fonts

One way of improving the looks of this worksheet is to also right justify the text **Jan** and **Feb** within their respective cells. To do this, move the active cell to B3 and select the range B3 to C3 by dragging the mouse, then either click the **Align Right** button, shown here, or choose the **Format**, **Cells** command, then select the **Alignment** tab from the displayed Format Cells dialogue box, shown below, click the down-arrow against the **Horizontal** text box, highlight **Right** from the drop-down menu options, and press **OK**.

Fig. 7.14 Formatting Cells by Using the Alignment Tab Sheet.

No matter which method you choose, the text should now appear right justified within their cells. However, although the latter method is lengthier, it nevertheless provides you with greater flexibility in displaying text, both in terms of position and orientation.

We could further improve the looks of our worksheet by choosing a different font size for the heading **Project Analysis**. To achieve this, select cell A1, then click on the down arrow against the **Font Size** button on the Formatting Bar, to reveal the band of available point sizes for the selected font, as shown overleaf. From this band, choose 14, then click in succession the **Bold** and **Italic** buttons.

Finally, since the numbers in cells B4 to C4 represent money, it would be better if these were prefixed with the £ sign. To do this, select the cell range B4:C4, then either click the **Currency** button on the Formatting Bar, shown here, or choose the **Format, Style** command and select **Currency** from the list under **Style name** in the displayed Style dialogue box.

The numbers within the chosen range will now be displayed in currency form, and the width of the cells will automatically adjust to accommodate them, if they are too long which is the case in our example.

To see the actual new width of, say column C, place the mouse pointer, as shown, to the right of the column letter on the dividing line. When the mouse pointer changes to the shape shown here in Fig. 7.14, press the left mouse button without moving

Fig. 7.15 Formatting Numbers in Currency Style.

the mouse. The current width will then display within a pop-up text box as 79 pixels, increased from the default column width of 64 pixels.

This new width accommodates our numbers exactly, but we might like to increase it to, say, 82 pixels so that it looks better. To do this, place the mouse pointer in between the column letters, and drag the pointer to the right, until the width of the column displays as 82 pixels, which also happens to be 11 characters wide.

Saving a Workbook

Now, let us assume that we would like to stop at this point, but would also like to save the work entered so far before leaving the program. First, return to the Home position by pressing <Ctrl+Home>. This is good practice because the position of the cell pointer at the time of saving the file is preserved. For example, had you placed the cell pointer well beyond the data entry area of your worksheet at the time of saving, when you later opened this worksheet you might be confused to see empty cells surrounding the cell pointer - you might think that you have opened an empty worksheet.

Next, choose the **File, Save** command to reveal the Save As dialogue box. We will select to save our work in the folder we created within **My Documents** folder for our Office Word 2003 examples. If you have not created this folder already, please refer to page 91 to find out how to do it.

To save our work currently in memory, we selected the **Office 2003 Docs** folder in the **Save in** field of the Save As dialogue box, then moved the cursor into the **File name** box, and typed **Project 1**. We suggest you do the same.

Fig. 7.16 Creating a New Folder in the Save As Dialogue Box.

The file will be saved in the default file type *Microsoft Office Excel Workbook*, as displayed in the **Save as type** box. Excel adds the file extension **.xls** automatically and uses it to identify it.

By clicking the **Save as type** button at the bottom of the Save As dialogue box, you can save your work in a variety of other formats, including Web Page (html), Template, and earlier versions of Excel.

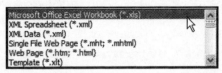

Fig. 7.17 Available Type Formats for Saving Work.

If you want to create backup files or provide password protection to your file, click the down-arrow against the **Tools** button at the top of the Save As dialogue box, and select **General Options** from the displayed drop-down menu. This opens the Save Options dialogue box, shown in the middle of the composite screen dump in Fig. 7.18. Fill in this dialogue box appropriately and press the **OK** button.

Fig. 7.18 The Save Options Dialogue Box.

Finally, pressing the **Save** button causes your work to be saved under the chosen filename.

Opening a Workbook

An already saved workbook, or file, can be opened by either clicking at the **Open** button, shown here, or selecting the **File, Open** command which displays the Open dialogue box. Excel asks for a filename to open, with the default *All Microsoft Office Excel Files* being displayed in the **Files of type** box, as shown in Fig. 7.19. If the file was saved, double-click the **Office 2003 Docs** folder and select it by clicking its name in the list box, then click the **Open** button.

Fig. 7.19 The Open Dialogue Box.

Fig. 7.20 The Look In box of the Open Dialogue Box.

If you haven't saved it, don't worry as you could just as easily start afresh.

If you want to change the logged drive, click the down-arrow against the **Look in** box, of the Open dialogue box, and select the appropriate drive from the drop-down list, as shown here for our computer. In your case, this list will most certainly be different.

If you have been working recently with an Excel file and have saved it, and you have just launched Excel, the name of the file together with those of other files you have looked up or worked with recently, will appear in the **New Workbook** Task Pane as shown in Fig. 7.21.

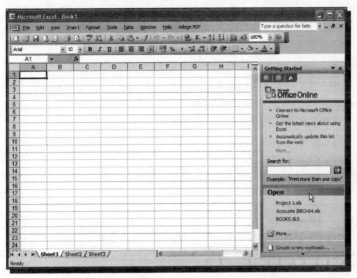

Fig. 7.21 The Task Pane List of Recently Used Files.

Exiting Excel

To exit Excel, close any displayed dialogue boxes by clicking the **Cancel** button, and make sure that the word **Ready** is displayed on the status bar (press the <Esc> key until it does), and either

- choose the **File, Exit** command,
- use the <Alt+**F4**> key combination, or
- click the **Close** button.

No matter which command you choose, if you have changed any opened worksheet, Excel will warn you and will ask for confirmation before exiting the program, as follows.

Fig. 7.22 Excel's File Save Warning Message.

If you do not want to save the changes, then press the **No** button, otherwise press **Yes**.

8

Filling in a Worksheet

We will use, as an example of how a worksheet can be built up, the few entries on 'Project Analysis' from the previous chapter. If you have saved **Project 1**, then either click its name in the Task Pane, click the **Open** button, or use the **File, Open** command, then highlight its filename in the Open dialogue box, and click the **OK** button. If you haven't saved it, don't worry as you could just as easily start afresh.

Next, either double-click on the contents of a cell to edit existing entries, or simply retype the contents of cells, so that your worksheet looks as near as possible to the one in Fig. 8.1. For formatting details, see below and the next page.

Fig. 8.1 Entering Data in Project 1 Worksheet.

The lines, like the double line stretching from A3 to E4 were entered by first selecting the cell range A3:E4, then clicking the down-arrow of the **Borders** button on the Formatting Bar, and selecting the appropriate border from the 12 displayed options.

Formatting Entries

The information in cell A1 (Project Analysis: Adept Consultants Ltd.) was entered left-justified and formatted by clicking on the **Font Size** button on the Formatting Bar, and selecting 14 point font size from the band of available font sizes, then clicking in succession the **Bold** and **Italic** buttons, shown to the left.

The text in the cell block B3:E3 was formatted by first selecting the range and then clicking the **Centre alignment** button on the Formatting Bar, so the text within the range was displayed centre justified.

The numbers within the cell block B4:E4 were formatted by first selecting the range, then clicking the **Currency** button on the Formatting Bar, shown here, so the numbers appeared with two digits after the decimal point and prefixed with the £ sign.

All the text appearing in column A (apart from that in cell A1) was just typed in (left justified), as shown in the screen dump in Fig. 8.1. The width of all the columns A to E was adjusted to 11 characters; a quick way of doing this is to select one row of these columns, then use the **Format, Column, Width** command, and type 11 in the displayed box.

Filling a Range by Example

To fill a range by example, select the first cell of a range,

point at the bottom right corner of the cell and when the mouse pointer changes to a small cross, drag the mouse in the required direction to fill the range.

In the above case, we started with a cell containing the abbreviation 'Jan'. The next cell to the right will automatically fill with the text 'Feb' (Excel anticipates that you want to fill cells by example with the abbreviations for months, and does it for you). Not only that, but it also copies the format of the selected range forward.

The Auto Fill Smart Tag

When you release the mouse button, Excel places a Smart Tag next to the end of the filled-in range. Clicking the down-arrow of this Smart Tag displays a drop-down menu of options, as shown in Fig. 8.2.

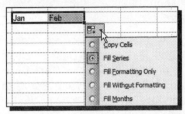

Fig. 8.2 The Auto Fill Smart Tag Options.

Entering Text, Numbers and Formulae

Excel allows you to format both text (labels) and numbers in any way you choose. For example, you can have numbers centre justified in their cells.

When text, a number, a formula, or an Excel function is entered into a cell, or reference is made to the contents of a cell by the cell address, then the content of the status bar changes from **Ready** to **Enter**. This status can be changed back to **Ready** by either completing an entry and pressing <Enter> or one of the arrow keys, or by pressing <Esc>.

We can find the 1st quarter total income from consultancy, by activating cell E4, typing

    =b4+c4+d4

and pressing <Enter>. The total first quarter income is added, using the above formula, and the result (£45,000) is placed in cell E4.

Now complete the insertion into the spreadsheet of the various amounts under 'costs' and then choose the **File, Save As** command to save the resultant worksheet under the filename **Project 2**, before going on any further. Remember that saving your work on disc often enough is a good thing to get used to, as even the shortest power cut can cause the loss of hours of hard work!

Using Functions

In our example, writing a formula that adds the contents of three columns is not too difficult or lengthy a task. But imagine having to add 20 columns! For this reason Excel has an inbuilt summation function which can be used to add any number of columns (or rows).

To illustrate how this and other functions can be used, activate cell E4 and first press <Del> to clear the cell of its formula, then click the **Insert Function** button, shown here, on the left of the Formula Bar. If the function you require appears on the displayed dialogue box under **Select a function**, choose it, otherwise type a brief description of what you want to do in the **Search for a function** text box and press **Go**, or select the appropriate class from the list under **Or select a category**.

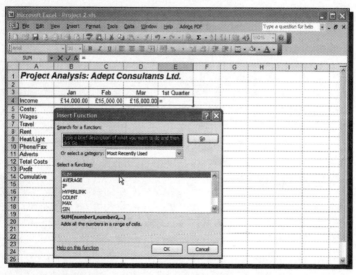

Fig. 8.3 Selecting a Function to Insert in a Cell.

Choosing the **SUM** function, inserts the entry SUM(B4:D4) in the Edit line, as shown in Fig. 8.4. Clicking the **OK** button, causes the result of the calculation of the chosen function to be entered in the selected worksheet cell.

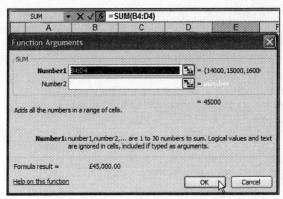

Fig. 8.4 The Function Arguments Dialogue Box.

Note that the arguments in the above case are given as B4:D4 in the **Number1** box and the actual result of the calculation is displayed next to it. Pressing the **OK** button, causes the function to be pasted into cell E4, but only the formula result is displayed in the cell. If you click in the **Number2** box you can select another cell range to be summed. The overall result appears at the bottom of the box.

Using the AutoSum Button

With addition, there is a better and quicker way of letting Excel work out the desired result. To illustrate this, select the cell range B6:E12, which contains the 'Costs' we would like to add up. To add these in both the horizontal and vertical direction, we include in the selected range an empty column to the right of the numbers and an empty row below the numbers, as shown in fig. 8.5.

	A	B	C	D	E	F
1	*Project Analysis: Adept Consultants Ltd.*					
2						
3		Jan	Feb	Mar	1st Quarter	
4	Income	£14,000.00	£15,000.00	£16,000.00	£45,000.00	
5	Costs:					
6	Wages	2000	3000	4000		
7	Travel	400	500	600		
8	Rent	300	300	300		
9	Heat/Light	150	200	130		
10	Phone/Fax	250	300	350		
11	Adverts	1100	1200	1300		
12	Total Costs					
13	Profit					
14	Cumulative					
15						

Fig. 8.5 Selecting a Range to be Summed.

Σ ▾   Pressing the **AutoSum** button, shown here, inserts
the result of the summations in the empty column and
row, as shown in Fig. 8.6. The selected range remains
selected so that any other formatting can be applied by
simply pressing the appropriate icon button.

Fig. 8.6 Using the AutoSum Toolbar Button on a Selected Range.

Note that the **AutoSum** button now has a down-arrow to the
right of it. Clicking this arrow, displays
a list of alternative options, as shown
here. From this list you can choose to
calculate the **Average**, **Count** the
entries, find the **Max** or **Min** values in
a row or column, or indeed display the
Insert   Function   dialogue   box
discussed earlier and shown in Fig.
8.3 by selecting the **More Functions**
option.

Fig. 8.7 The AutoSum
Menu.

Now   complete   the   insertion   of
formulae in the rest of the worksheet, noting that 'Profit', in
B13, is the difference between 'Income' and 'Total Cost',
calculated by the formula **=b4-b12**. To complete the entry,
this formula should be copied using the 'fill by example'
method we discussed earlier, into the three cells to its right.

The 'Cumulative' entry in cell B14 should be a simple reference to cell B13, that is **=b13**, while in cell C14 it should be **=b14+b13**. Similarly, the latter formula is copied into cell D14 using the 'fill by example' method.

Next, format the entire range B6:E12 by selecting the range and clicking the **Currency** button.

If you make any mistakes and copy formats or information into cells you did not mean to, use the **Edit, Undo** command or click the **Undo** button which allows you to selectively undo what you were just doing. To blank the contents within a range of cells, first select the range, then press the <Del> key.

The worksheet, up to this point, should look like the one in Fig. 8.8 below.

Fig. 8.8 The Completed 1st Quarter Worksheet.

Finally, use the **File, Save As** command to save your work under the filename **Project 3** in the **Office 2003 Docs** folder.

Printing a Worksheet

To print a worksheet, make sure that the printer you propose to use was defined when you first installed Windows.

If you have named more than one printer in your original installation of Windows, and want to select a printer other than your original first choice, then select the **File, Print** (or <Ctrl+P> command, click the down-arrow against the **Name** box on the displayed Print dialogue box and select the required printer, as shown in Fig. 8.9.

Fig. 8.9 The Print Dialogue Box.

If you want to change the paper size, print orientation or printer resolution, click the **Properties** button on the Print dialogue box. These and other changes to the appearance of the printout can also be made by choosing the **File, Page Setup** command which displays the Page Setup dialogue box, as shown in Fig. 8.10 on the next page.

Fig. 8.10 The Page Setup Dialogue Box.

By selecting the appropriate Tab on this dialogue box, you can change your **Page** settings, page **Margins**, specify a **Header/Footer**, and control how a **Sheet** should be printed. Each Tab displays a different dialogue box, appropriate to the function at hand. In the **Header/Footer** dialogue box you can even click the down-arrow against the Header and Footer boxes to display a suggested list for these, appropriate to the work you are doing, the person responsible for it and even the date it is being carried out! Try it.

A very useful feature of Excel is the **Scaling** facility shown in the above dialogue box. You can print actual size or a percentage of it, or you can choose to fit your worksheet on to one page which allows Excel to scale your work automatically.

To preview a worksheet, click the **Print Preview** button on the extension of the Standard Toolbar, shown here - once this is done the button is transferred on to the Standard Toolbar next to the **Print** button, or click the **Print Preview** button on the Page Setup dialogue box, or the **Preview** button on the Print dialogue box. You can even use the **File, Print Preview** command!

The idea of all these preview choices is to make it easy for you to see your work on screen before committing it to paper, thus saving even a few more trees!

Enhancing a Worksheet

You can make your work look more professional by adopting various enhancements, such as single and double line cell borders, shading certain cells, and adding meaningful headers and footers.

However, with Excel you can easily select a predefined style to display your work on both the screen and on paper. To do this, place the active cell within the table (or range) you want to format, say C5, then select the **Format, AutoFormat** which will cause the following dialogue box to appear on the screen, displaying a sample of the chosen table format. In this way you can choose what best suits your needs. We selected 'Classic 2' and pressed **OK**.

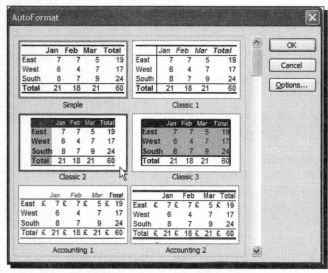

Fig. 8.11 The AutoFormat Dialogue Box.

Next, reduce the title of the worksheet to 'Project Analysis', then centre it within the range A1:E1, by first selecting the range, then clicking the **Merge and Centre** button, shown here, which centres the title within the specified range. Finally, save the worksheet as **Project 4**, before going on.

Header and Footer Icons and Codes

With the help of header and footer icons and their codes, shown below, you can position text or automatically insert information at the top or bottom of a report printout.

To add a header to our printed example, use the **File, Page Setup** command and click first the **Header/Footer** Tab, then the **Custom Header** button and type the information displayed below in the **Left section** and **Right section** of the Header box.

Fig. 8.12 The Header Dialogue Box.

While the insertion pointer is in, say, the **Center section** of the Header box, pointing and clicking on the **Sheet Name** button, inserts the &[Tab] code which has the effect of inserting the sheet name of the current active sheet at the time of printing. The first icon button displays the Font dialogue box, while the others display the following codes:

Code	*Action*
&[Page]	Inserts a page number.
&[Pages]	Inserts the total number of pages.
&[Date]	Inserts the current date.
&[Time]	Inserts the current time.
&[File]	Inserts the filename of the current workbook.

Setting a Print Area

To choose a smaller print area than the current worksheet, select the required area by highlighting the starting cell of the area and dragging the mouse, or using the **<Shift+Arrows>**, to highlight the block, and use the **File, Print** command which displays the dialogue box in Fig. 8.13.

Fig. 8.13 Printing a Selection Area.

Choose the **Selection** button in the **Print what** box, and either click the **Preview** or the **OK** button to preview your report on screen or print it on paper. When in preview mode, the following buttons are available to you.

Fig. 8.14 A Selection Area in Print Preview.

The first two allow you to change sheets, while the next one allows you to review your print output magnified or at full page size - when in full page size, the mouse pointer looks like a magnifying glass. The next four buttons can be used to print, change page settings, display and change the margins, or adjust the page size by dragging the page breaks to a new position. To return to normal view, click the **Close** button.

Another way to set the area to print is to select it first, then use the **File, Print Area, Set Print Area** menu command. To print selected sheets or the entire workbook, click the appropriate button in the **Print what** box of the Print dialogue box.

The default selection in the **Print what** box is **Active sheet(s)** which is also what will be printed out if you click the **Print** button, shown here. If you have included headers and footers, these will be printed out irrespective of whether you choose to print a selected range or a selected worksheet. To centre the page horizontally on the paper, use the **File, Page Setup** command, click the Margins tab and select the option. Finally, previewing our worksheet, produced the screen in Fig, 8.15 in which we show how you can fine-tune the margins so that the worksheet is centred on the page:

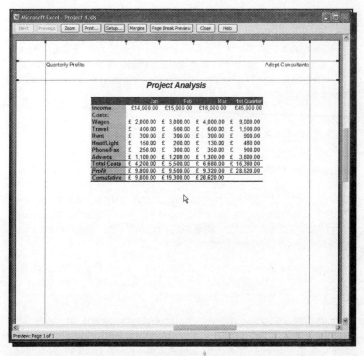

Fig. 8.15 Changing the Margins of a Report Page Preview.

3-Dimensional Worksheets

In Excel, a Workbook is a 3-dimensional file made up with a series of flat 2-dimensional sheets stacked 'on top of each other'. Each sheet is the same size, and in itself, behaves the same as the more ordinary worksheets. As mentioned previously, each separate sheet in a file has its own Tab identifier at the bottom of the screen. Ranges can be set to span several different sheets to build up 3-dimensional blocks of data. These blocks can then be manipulated, copied, or moved to other locations in the file. A cell can reference any other cell in the file, no matter what sheet it is on, and an extended range of functions can be used to process these 3-dimensional ranges.

Manipulating Ranges

The best way to demonstrate a new idea is to work through an example - we will use the worksheet saved under **Project 4**. Next, start Excel, use the **File, Open** command, or click the **File Open** button, and select **Project 4**. Pressing <Enter>, displays a worksheet similar to the one shown in Fig. 8.15.

Copying Sheets in a Workbook

We will now fill another three sheets behind the present one, in order to include information about ADEPT Consultants' trading during the other three quarters of the year. The easiest way of doing this is by copying the information in Sheet1, including the formatting and the entered formulae, onto the other three sheets, then edit the numerical information in these appropriately.

To simplify this operation, Excel has a facility which allows you to copy a sheet into a workbook. There are two ways of doing this: (a) with the mouse, or (b) using the menus.

With the mouse, make the sheet you want to copy the current sheet, then press the <Ctrl> key, and while keeping it pressed, point with the mouse on the Tab of Sheet1 and drag it to the right, as shown in Fig. 8.16.

Fig. 8.16 Copying a Sheet into a Workbook.

A small black triangle indicates the place where the copy will be inserted, as shown above. If you insert a copy, say before Sheet2, when you release the mouse button the inserted sheet will be given the name Sheet1(2), while inserting a second copy before Sheet2 will be given the name Sheet1(3). To delete a worksheet, right-click its tab and select **Delete** from the pop-up menu.

To copy a sheet with the menus, right-click the sheet, then select the **Move or Copy** command to display the dialogue box in Fig. 8.17. Next,

Fig. 8.17 Copying a Sheet.

highlight Sheet2 in the **Before sheet** list, check the **Create a copy** option at the bottom of the box, and click **OK**. Sheet1(2) will be inserted in the Workbook, in the above case.

When you have three copies placed, double-click the Tabs of Sheet1 and the three new sheets and change their names to 'Quarter 1', 'Quarter 2', 'Quarter 3' and 'Quarter 4', respectively, as shown in Fig. 8.18.

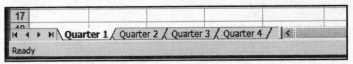

Fig. 8.18 Renaming the Tabs of Worksheets.

The correct contents of the second sheet should be as shown in Fig. 8.19 on the next page.

	A	B	C	D	E	
1	*Project Analysis 2nd Quarter*					
2						
3		Apr	May	Jun	2nd Quarter	
4	Income	£15,500.00	£16,000.00	£16,500.00	£48,000.00	
5	Costs:					
6	Wages	£ 3,500.00	£ 4,000.00	£ 4,500.00	£ 12,000.00	
7	Travel	£ 500.00	£ 550.00	£ 580.00	£ 1,630.00	
8	Rent	£ 300.00	£ 300.00	£ 300.00	£ 900.00	
9	Heat/Light	£ 150.00	£ 120.00	£ 100.00	£ 370.00	
10	Phone/Fax	£ 300.00	£ 350.00	£ 400.00	£ 1,050.00	
11	Adverts	£ 1,250.00	£ 1,300.00	£ 1,350.00	£ 3,900.00	
12	Total Costs	£ 6,000.00	£ 6,620.00	£ 7,230.00	£ 19,850.00	
13	*Profit*	£ 9,500.00	£ 9,380.00	£ 9,270.00	£ 28,150.00	
14	*Cumulative*	£ 9,500.00	£18,880.00	£28,150.00		
15						
16						

H ◄ ► H \ Quarter 1 \ **Quarter 2** / Quarter 3 / Quarter 4 / |◄

Ready

Fig. 8.19 The Data for the Second Quarter.

The easiest way to enter these 2nd Quarter results is to edit the copied data (from Quarter 1) by either using the EDIT key (**F2**), or double-clicking the cell you want to edit. You should now be in a position to complete editing this sheet. Be extra careful, from now on, to check the identification Tab at the bottom of the screen, so as not to get the sheets mixed up. You do not want to spend time editing the wrong worksheet!

After building up the four worksheets (one for each quarter - see below for details on the 3rd and 4th quarters) save the file as **Project 5**.

	Jul	Aug	Sep	Oct	Nov	Dec
Income	17,000	17,500	18,000	18,500	19,000	19,500
Costs:						
Wages	4,000	4,500	5,000	4,500	5,000	5,500
Travel	600	650	680	630	670	700
Rent	300	300	300	300	300	300
Heat/Light	50	80	120	160	200	250
Phone/Fax	350	380	420	400	420	450
Adverts	1,400	1,450	1,500	1,480	1,500	1,530

Linking Sheets

Use the **Insert**, **Worksheet** menu command to place a worksheet in front of our 'stack' of data sheets to show a full year's results. Next, make a copy of the 1st Quarter sheet and place it in the sheet in front of it, then delete the entries in columns B to E, and name it 'Consolidation'.

We will now link the consolidation sheet to the other quarterly data sheets so that the information contained on them is automatically summarised and updated on it. The quarter totals in columns E of sheets Quarter 1, Quarter 2, Quarter 3, and Quarter 4, can be copied in turn to the clipboard using the **Edit, Copy** command, and then pasted to the appropriate column of the Consolidation sheet using the **Edit, Paste Special** command and clicking the **Paste Link** button on the displayed dialogue box.

Note: Empty cells linked with this method, like those in cells E5 of each quarter, appear as 0 (zero) in the Consolidation sheet. These can be removed by highlighting them and pressing the <Delete> key. Do not check the **Skip blanks** box in the Paste Special dialogue box, as this greys out the **Paste Link** button and clicking **OK** gives the wrong result!

Next, insert appropriate formulae in row 14 to correctly calculate the cumulative values in the Consolidation sheet. The result should be as shown in Fig. 8.20. Finally, save the resultant workbook as **Project 6**.

Fig. 8.20 The Linked Data in a Consolidation Sheet.

Relative and Absolute Cell Addresses

Entering a mathematical expression into Excel, such as the formula in cell C14 which was

    =B14+C13

causes Excel to interpret it as 'add the contents of cell one column to the left of the current position, to the contents of cell one row above the current position'. In this way, when the formula was later copied into cell address D14, the contents of the cell relative to the left position of D14 (i.e. C14) and the contents of the cell one row above it (i.e. D13) were used, instead of the original cell addresses entered in C14. This is relative addressing.

To see the effect of relative versus absolute addressing, copy the formula in cell C14 into C17, as shown in Fig. 8.21.

Fig. 8.21 Demonstrating Relative and Absolute Cell Addressing.

Note that in cell C14 the formula was =B14+C13. However, when copied into cell C17 the formula appears as

```
=B17+C16
```

This is because it has been interpreted as relative addressing. In this case, no value appears in cell C17 because we are attempting to add two blank cells.

Now change the formula in C14 by editing it to

```
=$B$14+$C$13
```

which is interpreted as absolute addressing. Copying this formula into cell C17 calculates the correct result. Highlight cell C17 and observe the cell references in its formula; they have not changed from those of cell C14.

The $ sign must prefix both the column reference and the row reference. Mixed cell addressing is permitted; as for example when a column address reference is needed to be taken as absolute, while a row address reference is needed to be taken as relative. In such a case, the column letter is prefixed by the $ sign.

When building an absolute cell reference in a formula, it is easier to select each cell address within a formula by double-clicking on it with the left mouse button then, when selected, keep on pressing the **F4** key until the correct $ prefix is set.

Freezing Panes on Screen

Sometimes there might be too much information on screen and attempting to see a certain part of a sheet might cause the labels associated with that information to scroll off the screen.

To freeze column (or row) labels of a worksheet on screen, move the cell pointer to the right (or below) the column (or row) which you want to freeze, and use the **Window, Freeze Panes** command. Everything to the left of (or above) the cell pointer will freeze on the screen.

To unfreeze panes, use the **Window, Unfreeze Panes** command.

The Paste Smart Tag

Note that in Fig. 8.21, when you try to **Paste** the contents of a cell (or range of cells), Excel displays a Smart tag at the bottom right corner of the cell in which you are about to paste data. When the mouse pointer is placed on this tag, a down-arrow appears next to it which when clicked opens up a menu of the most useful paste features you can use with that type of data, as shown in Fig. 8.22.

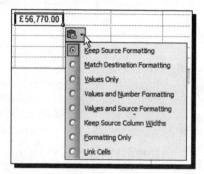

Fig. 8.22 The Paste Smart Tag
Menu Options.

In our case, the default, **Keep Source Formatting**, selection is what we need.

9

Spreadsheet Charts

Excel allows information within a worksheet to be represented in graphical form, which makes data more accessible to non-expert users who might not be familiar with the spreadsheet format. The saying 'a picture is worth a thousand words', applies equally well to charts and figures.

The package allows the use of several chart and graph types, including area, bar, column, line, doughnut, radar, XY, pie, combination, and several 3-D options of these charts. In all, Excel allows fourteen different types of charts, with almost 100 predefined formats, which can be selected by using the appropriate icon. These are made available to you once you have selected the data you want to chart and clicked on the **Chart Wizard** button on the toolbar.

Charts (you can have several per worksheet) can be displayed on screen at the same time as the worksheet from which they were derived, since they appear in their own 'chart' frame and can be embedded anywhere on a worksheet. Furthermore, they can be sent to an appropriate output device, such as a plotter or printer. Although this charting module rivals a standalone graphics package, and one could write a separate book on it, an attempt will be made to present its basics, in the space available within this book.

Preparing for a Column Chart

In order to illustrate some of the graphing capabilities of Excel, we will now plot the income of the consulting company we discussed in the **Project 6** file. However, before we can go on, you will need to complete the entries for the last two quarters of trading of the Adept Consultants' example, if you haven't already done so - see end of previous chapter.

Next, link the quarterly totals to the consolidation sheet, calculate the year's total, as shown in Figure 9.1, and save the resultant workbook as **Project 7**, before going on.

	F4		f_x =SUM(B4:E4)				
	A	B	C	D	E	F	G
1	*Project Analysis - Year Summary*						
2							
3		1st Quarter	2nd Quarter	3rd Quarter	4th Quarter	Total	
4	Income	£45,000.00	£48,000.00	£52,500.00	£57,000.00	£202,500.00	
5	Costs:						
6	Wages	£ 9,000.00	£12,000.00	£13,500.00	£ 15,000.00	£49,500.00	
7	Travel	£ 1,500.00	£ 1,630.00	£ 1,930.00	£ 2,000.00	£7,060.00	
8	Rent	£ 900.00	£ 900.00	£ 900.00	£ 900.00	£3,600.00	
9	Heat/Light	£ 480.00	£ 370.00	£ 250.00	£ 610.00	£1,710.00	
10	Phone/Fax	£ 900.00	£ 1,050.00	£ 1,150.00	£ 1,270.00	£4,370.00	
11	Adverts	£ 3,600.00	£ 3,900.00	£ 4,350.00	£ 4,510.00	£16,360.00	
12	Total Costs	£16,380.00	£19,850.00	£22,080.00	£ 24,290.00	£82,600.00	
13	*Profit*	£28,620.00	£28,150.00	£30,420.00	£ 32,710.00	£119,900.00	
14	*Cumulative*	£28,620.00	£56,770.00	£87,190.00	£119,900.00		
15							

Fig. 9.1 The Year's Consolidated Worksheet of Adept Consultants.

Now we need to select the range of the data we want to graph. The range of data to be graphed in Excel does not have to be contiguous for each graph, as with some other spreadsheets. With Excel, you select your data from different parts of a sheet with the <Ctrl> key pressed down. This method has the advantage of automatic recalculation should any changes be made to the original data. You could also collect data from different sheets to one 'graphing' sheet by linking them as we did with the consolidation sheet.

If you don't want the chart to be recalculated when you do this, then you must use the **Edit, Copy** and **Edit, Paste Special** commands and choose the **Values** option from the displayed dialogue box, which copies a selected range to a specified target area of the worksheet and converts formulae to values. This is necessary, as cells containing formulae cannot be pasted directly since it would cause the relative cell addresses to adjust to the new locations; each formula would then recalculate a new value for each cell and give wrong results.

The Chart Wizard

To obtain a chart of 'Income' versus 'Quarters', select the data in cell range A3..E4, then either click the **Chart Wizard** button, shown here, or use the **Insert, Chart** command. The Chart Wizard then opens the first of four dialogue boxes, as shown below, which guide you through the process.

Fig. 9.2 The First Chart Wizard Dialogue Box.

Now select the 3-D Column type and click the **Next >** button at the bottom of the displayed Chart Wizard dialogue box. The second dialogue box is then displayed as shown in Fig. 9.3 on the next page, after clicking the **Columns** radio button pointed to.

The third Chart Wizard dialogue box allows you to give a title to your chart (Income per Quarter in this case) and annotate the x- and y-axes, while the fourth dialogue box allows you to place the chart either on a separate sheet or on the sheet that was active when you first started the charting process - we chose the latter. On pressing the **Finish** button the chart shown in Fig. 9.4 should appear on your worksheet.

Fig. 9.3 A 3-D Columnar Income Chart.

Fig. 9.4 The Income per Quarter Columnar Chart.

Note that to find out the exact details of a given column on a chart, you need only place the mouse pointer on it to open a banner with the desired information.

While the frame containing a chart is selected (you can tell from the presence of the small black squares around it), you can change its size by dragging the small two-headed arrow pointer (which appears when the mouse pointer is placed on the small black squares of the frame). You can also move the frame and its contents to another position on the worksheet by pointing to the chart area, pressing and keeping depressed the left mouse button until the pointer changes to a small four-headed arrow shape, then dragging the changed mouse pointer to a new position.

Now select the chart frame, then use the **View**, **Toolbars** menu command and choose the **Chart** option from the sub-menu to display the Chart Toolbar shown in Fig. 9.5. You can use this toolbar to change to a different chart object, format the selected chart object, change the chart type, turn on/off the chart legend, turn on/off the selected data table for the chart, redraw the chart by row or column, and angle selected chart objects clockwise or anticlockwise. In fact, everything that you need to do to a chart is available right there on this Chart Toolbar.

Fig. 9.5 The Chart Toolbar.

As an example of what you can do with a chart, first select the object 'Chart Area', then either click the **Format Chart Area** button on the Chart Toolbar, double-click within the chart area or use the **Format, Selected Chart Area** command. Using any one of these three procedures displays the dialogue box in Fig. 9.6 shown on the next page.

Fig. 9.6 The Format Chart Area Dialogue Box.

From this dialogue box you can choose a pattern to be used as a frame, by selecting **Custom** under the Patterns tab and choose the 8th **Style**, the 4th **Weight** line, check the **Sha_dow** box and press **OK**.

Try it, then change the May income (on the Quarter 2 sheet) from £16,000 to £26,000, and watch how the change is reflected on the redrawn graph on the Consolidation sheet displayed below.

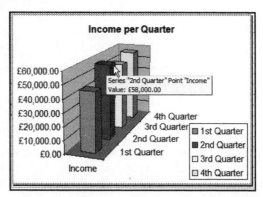

Fig. 9.7 The Formatted and Redrawn Income Chart.

Finally, revert to the original entry for the May income, change your chart back to a simple column type, and then save your work again under the filename **Project 7** by simply pressing the **Save** button shown here. Your current work will be saved to disc replacing the previous version under the same filename.

When Excel creates a chart, it plots each row or column of data in the selected range as a 'data series', such as a group of bars, lines, etc. A chart can contain many data series, but Excel charts data according to the following rules:

1.   If the selected range contains more rows than columns of data, Excel plots the data series by columns.

X-axis labels   1st data series   2nd data series   3rd data series

2.   If the selected range contains more columns than rows of data, or the same number of columns and rows, Excel plots the data series by rows.

Legend   X-axis labels
labels   1st data series
2nd data series

If you select a range to chart which includes column and row headings, and text above or to the left of the numeric data, Excel uses the text to create the axis labels, legends, and title.

If your data selection does not obey these rules, you must tell Excel how your data series is structured in the 2nd Chart Wizard dialogue box.

Editing a Chart

The easiest way to edit a chart is to right-click it within the chart area, but near its outer rim. This displays the shortcut menu shown in Fig. 9.8 on the next page.

As a chart is made up of several objects, for example, data series, plot area, the various axis data areas, legends, and chart area, you will get a different shortcut menu if you were pointing to these different areas. Try it. As you right-click different areas, their name will appear in the 'Name box' which is situated below the 'Font' box. The shortcut menu shown in Fig. 9.8 is the one you will get when you right-click the 'Chart Area'.

We have already used the first menu option to format our chart. The second menu option allows you to quickly change the chart type, while the third option can be used to change the source data. The fourth menu option allows you to add Titles, change axes, add grid lines and data labels, while the fifth option lets you specify whether you want your chart to be located in a new sheet or where you created it.

Fig. 9.8 The Chart Area
Shortcut Menu.

Saving Charts

When you save a workbook, the chart or charts you have created are saved with it. It is, therefore, a good idea not only to give each chart a title (by using **Chart Options** in the above shortcut menu - Fig. 9.8), but to also locate it on a differently named sheet.

To put the chart on a separate sheet, use the **Location** option in Fig. 9.8 and give it the name **Income Column**, as shown in Fig. 9.9.

Fig. 9.9 Changing the Chart Location.

Finally, save the workbook under the filename **Project 8**.

Predefined Chart Types

To select a different type of chart, click the **Chart Wizard** button shown here, or select the **Insert, Chart** command. The 1st Chart Wizard dialogue box displayed previously, lists 14 different chart options. These chart-types are normally used to describe the following relationships between data:

Area: for showing a volume relationship between two series, such as production or sales, over a given length of time.

Bar: for comparing differences in data (noncontinuous data that are not related over time) by depicting changes in horizontal bars to show positive and negative variations from a given position.

Bubble: for showing a type of XY (scatter) chart. The size of the data (radius of the bubble) indicates the value of a third variable.

Column: for comparing separate items (noncontinuous data which are related over time) by depicting changes in vertical bars to show positive and negative variations from a given position.

Cone: for showing 3-D column and bar charts in a more dramatic way.

Cylinder: similar to Cone.

Doughnut: for comparing parts with the whole. Similar to pie charts, but can depict more than one series of data.

☒	**Line:**	for showing continuous changes in data with time.
◕	**Pie:**	for comparing parts with the whole. You can use this type of chart when you want to compare the percentage of an item from a single series of data with the whole series.
♠	**Pyramid:**	similar to Cone.
⬠	**Radar:**	for plotting one series of data as angle values defined in radians, against one or more series defined in terms of a radius.
◿	**Surface:**	for showing optimum combinations between two sets of data, as in a topographic map. Colours and patterns indicate areas that are in the same range of values.
▦	**Stock:**	for showing high-low-close type of data variation to illustrate stock market prices or temperature changes.
⣿	**XY (Scatter):**	for showing scatter relationships between X and Y. Scatter charts are used to depict items which are not related over time.

You can change the type of chart by selecting one of the fourteen offered when the **Chart Type** button is clicked on the Chart Toolbar, as shown in Fig. 9.10.

Fig. 9.10 Changing the Chart Type.

Customising a Chart

To customise a chart, you need to know how to add legends, titles, text labels, arrows, and how to change the colour and pattern of the chart background, plot areas and chart markers, and how to select, move and size chart objects.

Drawing a Multiple Column Chart

As an exercise, we will consider a new column chart which deals with the quarterly 'Costs' of Adept Consultants. To achieve this, first select the Consolidation sheet of workbook **Project 8**, then highlight the cell range A3:E3, press the <Ctrl> key, and while holding it down, use the mouse to select the costs range A6:E11.

Next, click the **Chart Wizard** button, select Column from the **Chart type** list, click the fourth **Chart sub-type** option, and press the **Next** button. The 6 different quarterly costs will be drawn automatically, as displayed in the composite screen in Fig. 9.11, if the **Columns** radio button in the Second Wizard screen is selected.

Fig. 9.11 Creating the Costs Column Chart of Adept Consultants.

Because the selected range contains more rows than columns of data, Excel follows the 1st rule of data series selection which, however, might not be what you want.

To have the 'quarters' appearing on the x-axis and the 'costs' as the legends, we need to tell Excel that our data series is in rows by clicking the **Rows** button on the 2nd Chart Wizard dialogue box. Immediately this is done the column chart changes to:

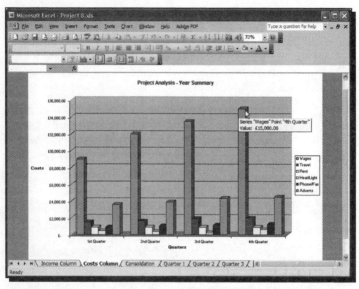

Fig. 9.12 The Adept Consultants Costs Shown in a Column Chart.

The chart title and axes titles were inserted by typing the heading 'Project Analysis - Year Summary' in the **Chart title** box of the 3rd Chart Wizard dialogue box, followed by the **Axis Titles** shown above.

Once you are satisfied with your efforts, click the **As new sheet** radio button of the 4th Chart Wizard dialogue box, and name your chart **Costs Column**. If you make a mistake and you want to try again, make sure the unwanted chart is selected, then press the <Del> key. Finally, save your work under the filename **Project 9**.

Changing a Title and an Axis Label

To change a title, an axis label, or a legend within a chart, click the appropriate area on the chart. This reveals that these are individual objects (they are surrounded by small black squares called 'handles') and you can edit, reposition, or change their font and point size. You can even rotate text within such areas in any direction you like. You could, of course, use the Chart Toolbar to achieve these changes.

To demonstrate these options, we will use the **Costs Column** chart saved in **Project 9**, so get it on screen if you are to follow our suggestions.

To change the font size of a chart title, click the Chart Title area to select it and double-click on the border that is displayed when you select it. Doing this, displays the Format dialogue box for the selected object, and clicking the Font tab reveals the contents of Fig. 9.13.

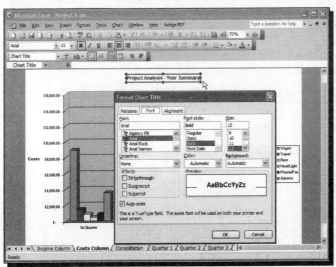

Fig. 9.13 Changing the Font Size of a Selected Object.

From here, we changed the font size of the chart title from 12 to 16 points. We also selected the Costs label and changed its size from 10 to 14 points, then clicked the Alignment tab to change its orientation to 90°, as shown in Fig. 9.14.

Fig. 9.14 Changing the Orientation of a Selected Object.

Drawing a Pie Chart

To change the chart type, simply select the chart, then click the Chart Wizard and choose the 3-D Pie chart from the displayed list. If the selected chart was the 'quarterly costs' chart, then clicking the **Next** button,   and clicking the **Columns** radio button, displays the chart type that would be redrawn for the specified data series, as shown in Fig. 9.15.

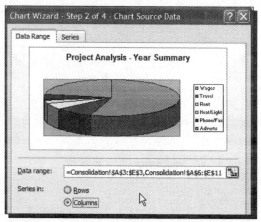

Fig. 9.15 Displaying Costs as a 3-D Pie Chart.

However, so as not to spoil your **Costs Column** chart, click the **Cancel** button at this stage.

To obtain a pie chart without spoiling the chart it is based on, you must select the data range again, then click the Chart Wizard, choose the pie chart from the displayed chart types, then select the specific pie chart that best fits your data, specify the type of series, and give the chart a title.

As a last example in chart drawing, we will use the data range A6:A11 and F6:F11 of the Consolidation worksheet to plot a 3-D pie chart. The steps are the same as before, but for the 3-D option and specifying the type of series data as 'columns'. Note that the chart title should now reflect the Year Totals, rather than the Quarter summaries. The result should be as shown in Fig. 9.16.

Fig. 9.16 Selecting Label Contents for a Pie Chart.

To display the above chart, we clicked the Data Labels tab and checked both the **Category name** and the **Percentage** check boxes in the 3rd dialogue box of the Chart Wizard.

This chart tells us, for example, that Wages for the whole year amount to 60% of the total yearly costs. Other cost categories are also displayed with their appropriate percentages. Clicking the **Finish** button displays the pie chart in its finished form, as shown overleaf in Fig. 9.17.

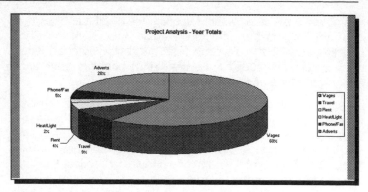

Fig. 9.17 A Pie Chart of the Yearly Total Costs of Adept Consultants.

Pointing to any pie slice, causes the pop-up poster to be displayed, informing you of the actual data series, its value and its percentage of the whole. It is now obvious that the information contained in this chart is much more than in the 2-D version.

If you want to explode an individual pie slice, you can do so by simply dragging it. This is possible as each slice is treated as a separate object, but you must increase the size of your chart before you can accurately pinpoint the required slice.

Finally, use the **Chart, Location** menu command to name this last version of the pie chart as **Costs Pie** and save your workbook.

* * *

Excel has many more features than the ones we have introduced in this book. For example, you could use Excel's database and macro capabilities, and also explore its various tools, such as the Goal Seek, Scenarios, Auditing, and Solver. We hope we have given you sufficient basic knowledge to be able to explore these topics by yourself.

However, if you would prefer to be guided through these topics, then may we suggest you keep a lookout for our forthcoming book *Microsoft Excel 2003 explained*, also to be published by BERNARD BABANI (publishing) Ltd., if demand justifies.

10

The PowerPoint Environment

Microsoft PowerPoint 2003 is a powerful and versatile Graphics Presentation package which deserves more attention than it gets from most users of Microsoft Office.

The key element of PowerPoint is the Slide Show and the production of ancillary material, such as scripted notes to accompany each slide, laser copies of slides, and an outline view of all the information in the presentation. However, Microsoft uses the word slide to refer to each individual page of a presentation and you can format the output for overhead projector acetates, or for electronic presentation on screen.

In addition, you can apply the skills you have already gained in using Word and Excel and use material created in these applications within PowerPoint.

New to PowerPoint 2003 is the ability to save your presentation and any linked files directly to a CD and use it on someone else's computer. The borrowed PC doesn't even have to have PowerPoint installed on it.

Starting the PowerPoint Program

PowerPoint is started in Windows either by clicking the *start* button then selecting **All Programs**, **Microsoft Office** and clicking on the Microsoft PowerPoint icon on the cascade menu, or by double-clicking on a PowerPoint presentation file. In the latter case the presentation will be loaded into PowerPoint at the same time. When you first start PowerPoint 2003 the program momentarily displays its opening screen, shown in Fig. 10.1, before displaying its first presentation document as shown in Fig. 10.2.

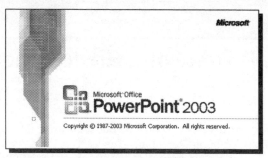

Fig. 10.1 PowerPoint's Opening Screen.

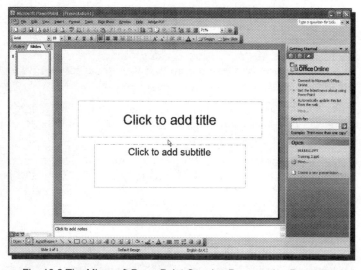

Fig. 10.2 The Microsoft PowerPoint Opening Presentation Document.

Whether you have used a previous version of PowerPoint or not, the first time you use the program, it might be a good idea to click the **Microsoft Office PowerPoint Help** button on the toolbar, then click the **Table of Contents** link on the **PowerPoint Help** Task Pane. This displays a list of help books, and clicking the first one opens a list of help topics as shown in Fig. 10.3 on the next page.

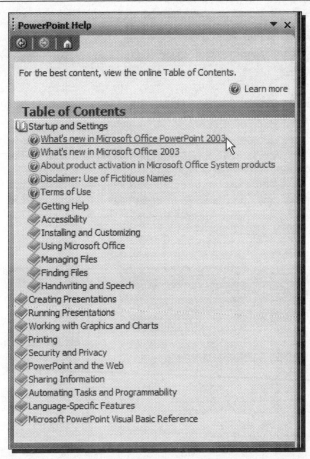

Fig. 10.3 The PowerPoint Help Screen.

Clicking the 'What's New in Microsoft PowerPoint 2003' link, pointed to in Fig. 10.3, opens a separate Help window with a list of additional topics. As you click each hypertext link, PowerPoint Help displays several topics on the subject which you might find helpful. We suggest you spend a little time here browsing through the various topics before going on. For additional information, click the **Learn more** button on the PowerPoint Help screen which will take you to mainly online topics. However, do investigate the 'Finding templates on your computer' link.

The PowerPoint Screen

When PowerPoint is loaded, a screen displays with similar Title bar, Menu bar, Toolbar and Formatting bar to those of Word and Excel. Obviously there are differences, but that is to be expected as PowerPoint serves a different purpose to the other programs.

The opening presentation screen of PowerPoint is shown in Fig. 10.4 below. The program follows the usual Microsoft Windows conventions with which you should be very familiar by now. Scroll bars and scroll buttons only appear within the window in which you load a presentation.

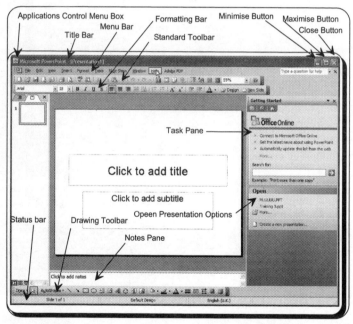

Fig. 10.4 The PowerPoint Opening Presentation Screen.

On the right of the opening presentation screen the Task Pane is displayed with listed options that make it easy for you to open an existing presentation, to start creating your presentation, or get presentation templates from the Web.

The **Open** section at the bottom of the **Getting Started** Task Pane (Fig. 10.4), allows you to open an existing presentation which might be listed, or go to the **Blank Presentation** Task Pane. Clicking the **More** icon, shown here, displays the Open dialogue box, as shown in Fig. 10.5, which also displays when you click the **Open** button on the Standard Toolbar, so that you can find and choose a presentation which might not be displayed in the **Open** list.

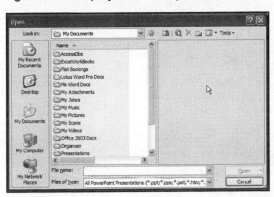

Fig. 10.5 The Open Presentation Dialogue Box.

Clicking the **Create a new presentation** link at the bottom of

the **Open** section, shown here, displays the **New Presentation** Task Pane, as shown in Fig. 10.6.

Under the **New** section of the pane, you have four options for creating a new presentation (see next page). In addition, you can also create a new presentation with the help of **Templates**, which can be found on Office Online, on your computer, or on your Web sites.

Fig. 10.6 The New Presentation Task Pane.

Creating New Presentations

The four options that allow you to create a new presentation, are as follows:

Blank Presentation

Allows you to start with a blank presentation with all values for colour scheme, fonts, and other design features set to default values. The same dialogue box also displays when you click the **New** button on the Standard Toolbar.

From Design Template

Allows you to select a presentation template that determines the colour scheme, fonts, and other design features of the presentation.

From AutoContent Wizard

Activates a Wizard that helps you determine the content and organisation of your presentation.

From Existing Presentation

Allows you to create a presentation based on an existing one.

The final link under this section of the Task Pane, allows you to create a photo album. Any presentations you currently have open in PowerPoint will not be affected by this task. A picture can be added to the photo album either from a file or disc, or from a camera or scanner.

Using the AutoContent Wizard

We will now use the AutoContent Wizard from the Task Pane to look for an existing presentation. Click this link to display the first of five Wizard screens, as shown in Fig. 10.7.

Fig. 10.7 Starting the AutoContent Wizard.

Clicking **Next**, displays the second Wizard screen (Fig. 10.8).

Fig. 10.8 Selecting the Type of Presentation.

For the type of presentation we selected **Projects**, then chose the second of the three projects displayed. Clicking **Next** displays the third Wizard screen, as shown in Fig. 10.9.

Fig. 10.9 Selecting Presentation Options.

Clicking the **Next** button displays the fourth Wizard screen which asks you to type in a title for the presentation - we typed   *Project Status*. Finally, clicking the **Finish** button displays the completed presentation shown in Fig. 10.10.

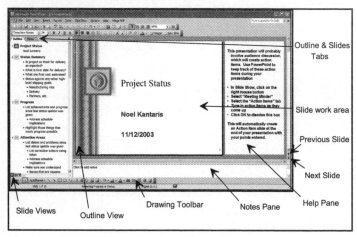

Fig. 10.10 The First of Ten Slides on Project Status.

PowerPoint Views

The Slide Views bar at the bottom left corner of the Presentation window together with the two tabs at the top of the left pane (see Fig. 10.10) are shown enlarged below.

Fig. 10.11 The Slide Views Bar and Controlling Tabs.

The three **Slide View** buttons are the key to the editing power of PowerPoint, while the two tabs control what you see in the left pane.

Normal View

The Normal view is the main editing view, which is used to write and design a presentation. The view has three working areas and a Help Pane (see Fig. 10.10): on the left, two tabs alternate between an outline view of your slide text and a thumbnails display of your slides; on the right, the slide pane, which displays a large view of the current slide; and on the bottom, the notes pane.

You can use these panes to work on all aspects of your presentation, and you can adjust their size by dragging their borders. The Outline and Slides tabs change to display an icon when the pane becomes narrow, and if you only want to see the current slide in the window as you edit, you can close the tabs with the Close box shown in Fig. 10.11.

The notes pane is used to add speaker notes or information you want to share with the audience. You can even have graphics in your notes, in which case you must add the notes in Notes Page View - use the **View, Notes Page** menu command.

The Outline and Slide Panes are also displayed when you save your presentation as a Web page.

Normal View - Outline Tab: In this view (Fig. 10.12), the
Outline Pane is enlarged for you to organise and edit your
presentation text.

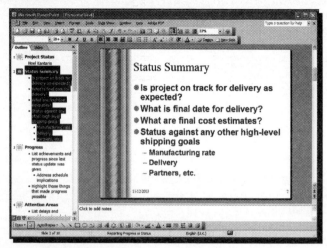

Fig. 10.12 The Outline Pane View of Project Status.

Normal View - Slides Tab: In this view (Fig. 10.13) the
Slides Pane allows you to see an enlarged slide area of a
selected slide.

Fig. 10.13 Slide View of Project Status.

Slide Sorter View

In this view (Fig. 10.14), you can see the whole presentation at once. You can reorder slides, add transitions, and set timing for electronic presentations. You can also select animated transitions for moving from slide to slide.

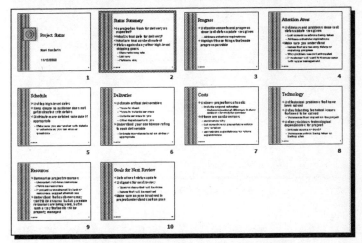

Fig. 10.14 Slide Sorter View of Project Status.

Notes Pages View

This is where you create speaker's notes which contain graphics for any or all of your presentation slides. To open up this view, use the **View, Notes Page** menu command.

As an example, we use the 2nd slide from our demonstration set, and imported a picture in the speaker's notes area, as shown in Fig. 10.15 on the next page. To do this, first type a line of text, similar to 'This is a test to see if a picture could be included', increase its font so that you can see it, then use the **Insert, Picture, From File** menu command, or click the **Insert Picture** button, shown here, on

 the Draw Toolbar, and select an appropriate picture from your Pictures folder (we will discuss this procedure in more detail in the next chapter).

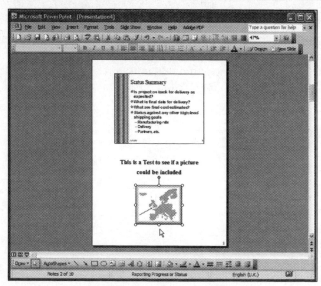

Fig. 10.15 The Speaker's Notes.

Drawing objects and pictures are not displayed in the notes pane (try it for yourself by using the **View, Normal** command), but appear when you work in Notes Page View or when you print slides with notes.

Slide Show View

In this view you see your work as an electronic presentation, with each slide filling the screen. You can also see the effect

of the transitions and timing that you set in the Slide Sorter View. To see the next slide in full-screen view either click the left mouse button or press the right cursor key. To return to a previous slide in full-screen view press the left cursor key. To return to a previous PowerPoint view from a full-screen view, press <Esc>, or click the right mouse button to display the menu (Fig. 10.16), and click **End Show**.

Fig. 10.16 The Slide Sorter View Quick Menu.

Preparing Speaker Notes

While preparing a presentation, you can make notes relating to each slide by right-clicking a slide while in full-screen view and selecting the **Speaker Notes** menu option, as shown in Fig. 10.17 below.

Fig. 10.17 The Meeting Minder Screen.

This displays the dialogue box shown in Fig. 10.18.

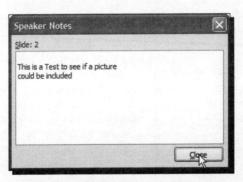

Fig. 10.18 The Speaker Notes Screen.

These notes can be printed and then used either to remember key points during a presentation, or to help the audience follow the presentation. Both the notes and handout pages have masters, where you can add items you want to appear on each page.

Setting Transitions, Animation and Timings

Your presentation will appear more professional if you set timings, transitions and animation. To do this, activate the Slide Sorter View and observe the extra Toolbar that appears to the right of the Standard Bar, as shown in Fig. 10.19.

Fig. 10.19 The Slide Sorter Toolbar.

Clicking the fifth button on the Slide Sorter Toolbar, displays the **Slide Transition** Task Pane, shown in Fig. 10.20. You can select a Transition Effect by choosing one from the list under **Apply to selected slides**. The effect will be seen on the slide which was selected at the time.

Now try the various options for yourself by, say, selecting *Shape circle* from the displayed list, then choosing *Camera* for sound under the **Modify transition**, check the 'Automatically after' box under **Advance slide** and select *00:03* for the timing, then click the **Apply to All Slides** button. The current effective timings will be displayed below each slide when in Slide Sorter View. Finally, click the **Slide Show** button to see all these options come to life. We hope you enjoy the show!

Fig. 10.20 The Slide Transition Pane.

The Slide Master

While a slide is selected, you can get a lot of help if you do the following:

- Click on the **Microsoft Office PowerPoint Help** button on the Toolbar to open its Help screen. In the 'Search for' box, type the string 'slide master', and click the ⊠ button.

- From the displayed list, select the third option 'About the slide master' which opens up the help window shown in Fig. 10.21, from which you can learn a lot.

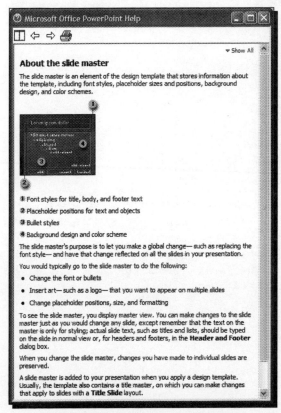

Fig. 10.21 The Help Screen on Slide Master.

In essence, each design template comes with its own slide master. The elements on the slide master control the design of the template, many of which have a separate title master.

When you apply a design template to a presentation, PowerPoint automatically updates the text styles and graphics on the slide master (use the **View, Master, Slide Master** command to see the one in Fig. 10.22), and changes the colour scheme to the one in the new design template.

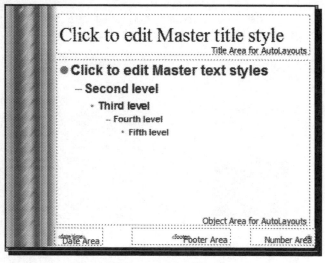

Fig. 10.22 Example of a Slide Master.

Any object you have added to the slide master, such as a text box or graphic, will not be deleted when you apply a new design template.

11

Designing a Presentation

In this chapter we will use PowerPoint's Wizards to design a simple presentation quickly and effectively. Below, we show the first page of the finished presentation in overhead format, so that you can have an idea of the overall design.

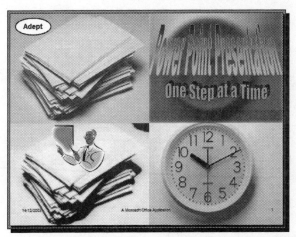

Fig. 11.1 The First Page of a Finished Presentation.

The AutoContent Wizard

When you first start PowerPoint, you are offered the opportunity to design a presentation using the AutoContent Wizard, select a template on which to base your work, begin with a blank presentation, or open an existing presentation.

Most users would, without question, like to produce a presentation in no time at all. The **AutoContent Wizard** is an excellent starting point, even if you know what you want to do and how to do it.

Later you can customise your presentation using PowerPoint's editing tools. But for now, click the down-arrow against the **Getting Started** pane and select the **New Presentation** option to open the Task Pane.

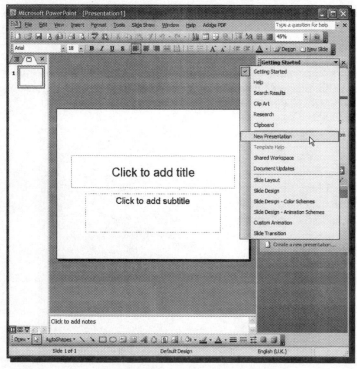

Fig. 11.2 Selecting the Type of Presentation.

On the **New Presentation** Task Pane, click the **From AutoContent wizard** link to start the display of five dialogue boxes in which you are:

- Provided with ideas and an organisation for your presentation.

- Asked to select the type of presentation you are going to give (we selected *Training*, as shown in Fig. 11.3 on the next page).

Fig. 11.3 Selecting the Type of Presentation.

It is possible that this feature might not be installed on your computer, in which case you will be asked to insert the Microsoft Office distribution disc in your CD-ROM drive so that files can be copied to your system. After this is done, you can continue with our example.

* You will be asked to specify what type of output you require (we selected *Color overheads*, as shown in Fig. 11.4).

Fig. 11.4 Selecting Type of Output.

- You will be asked for the title of your presentation (we typed *PowerPoint Presentation*, and *A Microsoft Office Application* for the footer, as shown in Fig. 11.5).

Fig. 11.5 Typing a Title and a Footer for the Presentation.

This is the only information required to create your presentation. Clicking the **Finish** button on the last dialogue box, creates it and displays it in Outline view complete with suggested topics, as shown in Fig. 11.6.

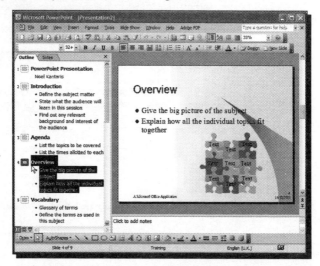

Fig. 11.6 Outline View of Selected Presentation.

The suggested topics of each slide can be changed to suit your needs, as shown below in Fig. 11.7. In this slide, we have added some extra demoted (more indented) topics by using the <Tab> key, and deleted topics (including objects) that were of no relevance to our presentation. To return to the original bullet level from a demoted level, use the <Shift+Tab> key.

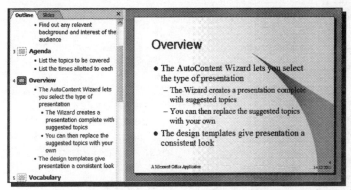

Fig. 11.7 The Changed Contents of a Slide.

The actual name of the person designing these slides that appears below the title of the 1st slide, is taken by PowerPoint automatically from information held on the *user* of the program. You could replace this by editing the relevant line when in Outline View (we typed here the text *One Step at a Time*).

Clicking the **Slide Sorter View** button at the bottom of the screen, displays all the slides in your presentation, as follows:

Fig. 11.8 Our Presentation in Slide Sorter View.

To move a slide to a different position in the set, simply left-click it and drag the modified pointer to the new position. Finally, save the result of your work so far under the filename **Training 1** in the **Office 2003 Docs** folder. PowerPoint inserts the three letter extension **.ppt**, to distinguish such files from others in the Office suite.

Selecting a Template

Our presentation might not look exactly what we had in mind, but we can select a different template to change the overall design. To change the default design of slides, first click the **Slide Sorter View** button, then do the following:

- Double-click the area at the bottom of the screen on the Status bar that holds the name of the current template (in our example this should read **Training**), or click the **Slide Design** button shown here. This opens the **Slide Design** Task Pane, shown in Fig. 11.9, for you to select a different presentation template.

Fig. 11.9 Selecting a Template.

Fig. 11.10 Selecting a
Template's Option.

- Select the **proposal.pot** template, click the down-arrow to the right of it, and choose **Apply to All Slides** option from the drop-down menu shown in Fig. 11.10.

What appears on your screen next, is the display of all your slides in the chosen template. Clicking the Slides tab, then the 1st slide, changes your display to that of Fig. 11.11. Clicking other slides, displays them in full size.

Fig. 11.11 Our Presentation Using the Proposal.pot Template.

Adding a Drawing to a Presentation

You can use the various buttons on the Drawing Toolbar at the bottom of the screen (if not activated use the **View, Toolbars, Drawing** command) to add to your presentation. The function of each Drawing tool will be described shortly.

To use the various Drawing tools, you must have a Presentation window open (we chose the 1st slide of our Training example for the display of our drawing). If you want your drawing to occur in all subsequent slides, you should use the **View, Master, Slide Master** menu command and start your drawing on the displayed Master slide.

Below, we used the Oval tool, the Text Box tool, and the Fill Colour tool to produce the logo shown here, which we placed at the top left corner of the 1st slide of our presentation, as shown in Fig. 11.12.

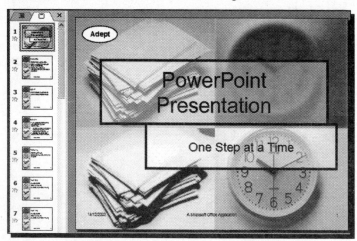

Fig. 11.12 Our Presentation with an Added Drawing.

You, of course, can use your drawing skills to produce your own logo. Save your creation under **Training 2**.

The Drawing Toolbar

The various functions offered by the Drawing Toolbar (see Fig. 11.13) are shared by all Office XP applications and give PowerPoint a superior graphics capability. Amongst the many features available are:

AutoShapes – the additional AutoShape categories, such as connectors, block arrows, flowchart symbols, stars and banners, callouts, and action buttons make drawing diagrams much easier.

Bezier curves – used to easily create exact curves with pinpoint precision.

3-D effects – allow you to transform 2-D shapes into realistic 3-D objects with new 3-D effects, such as changing the lighting perspective of a 3-D object.

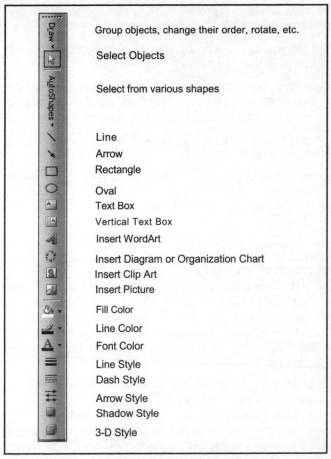

Group objects, change their order, rotate, etc.

Select Objects

Select from various shapes

Line
Arrow
Rectangle

Oval
Text Box
Vertical Text Box
Insert WordArt

Insert Diagram or Organization Chart
Insert Clip Art
Insert Picture

Fill Color
Line Color
Font Color

Line Style
Dash Style

Arrow Style
Shadow Style

3-D Style

Fig. 11.13 The Drawing Toolbar Buttons.

Perspective shadows – allow you to select from a wide range of shadows with perspective, and you can adjust the depth and angle of each shadow to make pictures more realistic.

Connectors – used to create diagrams and flowcharts with new straight, angled, and curved connectors between the shapes; when shapes are moved, the connectors remain attached and automatically reposition themselves.

Arrowhead styles – allow you to change the width and height of arrowheads for maximum effect.

Object alignment – allows you to distribute and space objects evenly, both horizontally and vertically.

Precise line-width control – allows you increased control over the width of lines by selecting pre-set options or customised line widths.

Image editing – lets you easily adjust the brightness or contrast of a picture.

Transparent background – allows you to insert a bitmap on your slides or Web pages that appears to be part of the design by turning background colours into transparent areas.

Inserting WordArt

The title and subtitle in Fig. 11.12 look rather severe in their heavy frames, so we will use WordArt to make them a bit more jazzy. To do this, first click each object (title and subtitle and press the <Delete> key - you will have to do this twice for each object, once to remove the typed words and a second time to remove the text box.

Next, click the **Insert WordArt** button, shown here, on the Drawing Toolbar. This opens the Microsoft WordArt Gallery, shown in Fig. 11.14, from which you can choose how you would like your title to be represented (we chose the one pointed to). Pressing the **OK** button opens the Edit WordArt Text box shown in Fig. 11.15 in which you type the title of your presentation. You will have to repeat this procedure for the subtitle, but choose a different WordArt image.

The final result, after scaling and moving the two text objects, is shown in Fig. 11.16 in which we also show the choices available when the **Character Spacing** button on the WordArt Toolbar is clicked. It is worthwhile spending some time here to familiarise yourself with the various options available on this Toolbar.

Fig. 11.14 The WordArt Gallery.

Fig. 11.15 The Edit WordArt Text Box.

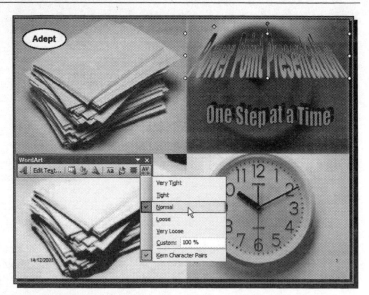

Fig. 11.16 Using the Options Available on the WordArt Toolbar.

Save the final presentation as **Training 3**. In the future, double-clicking on this file in a My Computer or Explorer window, will open PowerPoint with the file active.

Inserting a Picture or a Clip Art Image

A Picture or a Clip Art image can be inserted in a slide by using the appropriate buttons on the Drawing Toolbar. For example, in our case clicking the **Insert Picture** button shown here, opens the dialogue box in Fig. 11.17. This might be different for you, particularly if you are not running under Windows XP. Nevertheless, selecting a picture and pressing the **In<u>s</u>ert** button inserts the picture on your chosen slide.

To insert a Clip Art image, click the button shown here, to open the **Clip Art** Task Pane. Next, click the **Organize Clips** link at the bottom of the Task Pane, to open the Microsoft Clip Organizer window. Under the **Collection List**, choose **Office Collections**.

Fig. 11.17 The Insert Picture Dialogue Box.

This opens a further list of Clip Art sub-topics, as shown in Fig. 11.18 below, from which you can choose one to suit your needs.

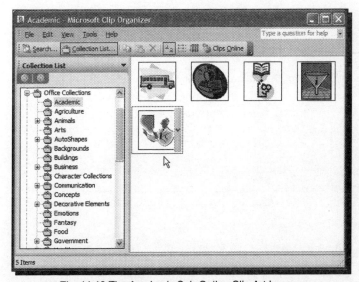

Fig. 11.18 The Academic Sub-Option Clip Art Images.

The Picture Bar

Should you want to change a picture or a Clip Art image you have inserted into your presentation, use the **View**, **Toolbars** menu command and select **Picture** from the drop-down menu. The Toolbar is shown in Fig. 11.19. The tools on this bar can be used to manipulate pictures to suit your needs. Their functions are as follows:

Insert Picture from File

Color

More Contrast

Less Contrast

More Brightness

Less Brightness

Crop

Rotate Left

Line Style

Compress Pictures

Recolor Picture

Format Picture

Set Transparent Color

Reset Picture

Fig. 11.19 The Picture Toolbar.

Let us try using these tools on an imported image to see how we can enhance or utterly destroy it! If, at the end of the day we don't save it, it doesn't matter what we do to it. So let us just experiment.

First, let us insert the Academic picture, pointed to in Fig. 11.8, and place it as shown in Fig. 11.20 below.

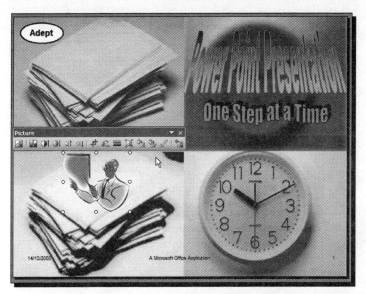

Fig. 11.20 Inserting the Academic Clip Art Image.

In the above screen dump, we have also superimposed the **Picture** Toolbar so that changes to it can be carried out quickly and easily. Try experimenting with the Contrast, the Brightness, and the Re-colour tools. If you don't like what you see, you can always use the Reset Picture tool. Our final efforts are shown in Fig. 11.1, shown at the beginning of this chapter. Obviously, subtle changes can not be detected in grey scale, but you will have the benefit of your colour screen. Have fun!

Packaging a Presentation on CD

To package a presentation on CD, so it can be used on a borrowed computer which doesn't have PowerPoint installed on it, is very easy indeed.

To illustrate the method, start PowerPoint and open the **Training 4** file. Next, use the **File**, **Pac̲kage for CD** menu command which displays the dialogue box shown in Fig. 11.21 below.

Fig. 11.21 The Package for CD
Dialogue Box.

Give your CD a name (PresentationCD is offered as a default) and click the **Copy to CD** button. To make quite sure what you copy to the CD is what you want, it might be a good idea to first use the **Copy to F̲older** button. To test your presentation, use **My Computer** to locate the PresentationCD folder, click on it to open it, and double-click the **play.bat** file to start your presentation.

* * *

PowerPoint is obviously capable of a lot more than we have introduced here, but you should now have the confidence to explore more of the package by yourself.

* * *

12

Microsoft Publisher 2003

Microsoft Publisher is a desktop publishing program that allows you to quickly and easily create great-looking results that you can print on either your own printer, a commercial printer, or publish on the World Wide Web.

You can use Publisher to either design a publication from scratch with a variety of blank page templates whose margins and folds are already laid out for you, or use one of several Wizards that help you add your own contents to professionally designed templates under different categories. There are Wizards that help you create common types of publications, such as Newsletters, Brochures, Postcards, and Web sites, to mention but a few, with each type of publication offering different designs that you can choose from.

Whichever method you use, the program provides you with ease of use, and advanced desktop publishing features, including the ability to select a variety of colour schemes. In addition, you can put to use all the skills gained in Microsoft Word to create professional looking output.

Starting the Publisher Program

Publisher is started in Windows either by clicking the *start* button then selecting **All Programs**, **Microsoft Office** and clicking on the **Microsoft Office Publisher** icon on the cascade menu, or by double-clicking on a Publisher document file. In the latter case the document will be loaded into Publisher at the same time. When you start Publisher 2003 the program momentarily displays its opening screen, shown in Fig. 12.1, before displaying a page with available designs for your new publication (more about this shortly) shown in Fig. 12.2.

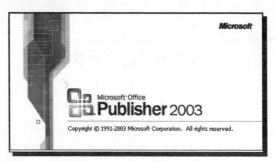

Fig. 12.1 Publisher's Opening Screen.

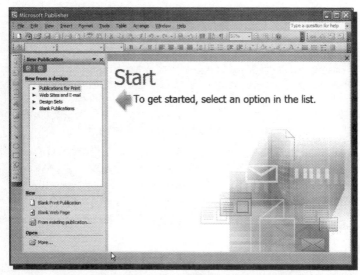

Fig. 12.2 The Microsoft Publisher Available Designs.

Whether you have used a previous version of Publisher or not, the first time you use the program, it might be a good idea to click the **Microsoft Office Publisher Help** button on the toolbar, then click the **Table of Contents** link on the **Publisher Help** Task Pane. This displays a list of help books, and clicking the first one opens a list of help topics as shown in Fig. 12.3 on the next page.

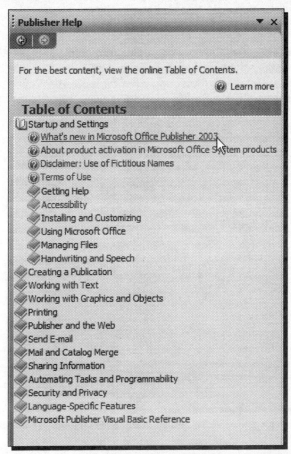

Fig. 12.3 The Publisher Help Screen.

Clicking the 'What's New in Microsoft Office Publisher 2003' link, pointed to in Fig. 12.3, opens a separate Help window with a list of additional topics. As you click each hypertext link, Publisher Help displays several topics on the subject which you might find helpful. We suggest you spend a little time here browsing through the various topics before going on. For additional information, click the **Learn more** button on the Publisher Help screen which will take you to mainly online topics. However, do investigate the 'Finding templates on your computer' link.

Creating a Publication

When you start Publisher the program displays a list of New Publications designs in the Task Pane on the left of the screen (Fig. 12.2). Selecting the first item, **Publications for Print**, reveals a sub-menu and the available designs under each entry, when selected, are displayed on the main panel of the screen, as shown in Fig. 12.4 for **Quick Publications**.

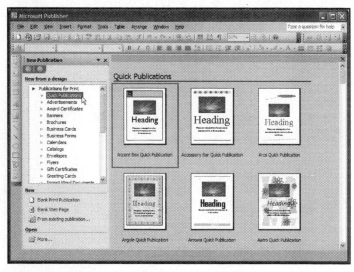

Fig. 12.4 The Available Designs in the Quick Publications Category.

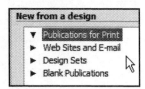

Fig. 12.5 Additional Design Options.

Note that under the **New from a design** entry at the top of the Task Pane of the Publisher screen, there are three additional choices, as shown here to the left. You can choose from designs for **Web Sites and E-mail**, **Design Sets**, or **Blank Publications**. Do have a look at all of these options before you start your own design - there are so many options that we are sure you will find one to suit your exact needs.

The first time you choose a specific design, double-click it to display the Personal Information dialogue box. If the selected design is not installed on your PC, you will be asked to insert the Office 2003 CD in your CD-ROM drive so that the necessary files can be copied to your computer.

In the Personal Information dialogue box, Publisher asks you to enter personal details, including company, position, name, address, etc., so they can be used to fill in certain types of publications, such as business cards, automatically.

Below we follow step-by-step what would happen had you selected, say, the Arcs Quick Publication, as shown in Fig. 12.6.

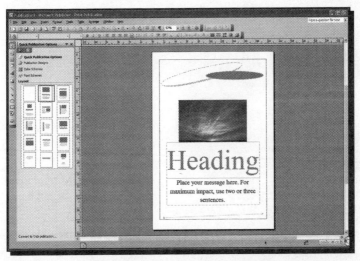

Fig. 12.6 Starting a Publications Wizard.

Note the listed options on the Task Pane. These allow you to select the following:

- The colour schemes of the page (not the graphic).
- The font schemes of the text on the page.

The available choice for the two options is shown in Fig. 12.7 on the next page.

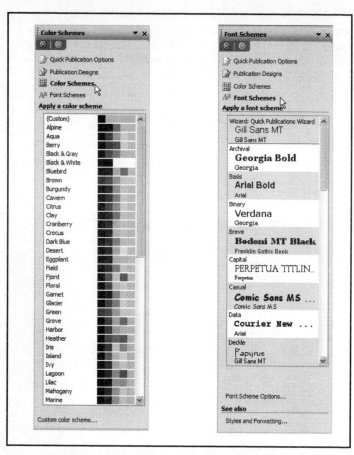

Fig. 12.7 Publisher's Colour and Font Schemes.

Having made a choice for colour and text fonts you will notice that as you place the mouse pointer on various parts of your selected design, the pointer changes to a 4-headed arrow with a flag below it telling you what object on the design you are about to move, as shown in Fig. 12.8.

Fig. 12.8 Moving an Object.

Finally, note the different menus and Toolbars that appear on your screen as you select different parts of your work. For example, selecting a Picture Frame, displays the Picture Bar (see page 232), and makes unavailable certain tools on the Formatting Bar (see page 78). When a Text Frame is selected, all the tools on the Formatting Bar become available. The respective effects on the Toolbars for the two selected objects are shown below in Fig. 12.9 and Fig. 12.10.

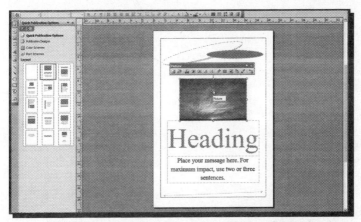

Fig. 12.9 The Toolbars when a Picture Frame is Selected.

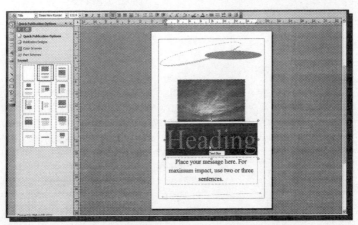

Fig. 12.10 The Toolbars when a Text Frame is Selected.

The Objects Tools

When a Picture or Text Frame is selected, the **Objects Tools** buttons display to the left of your screen. These buttons have the following functions:

Fig. 12.11 The Objects Toolbar.

Fig. 12.12 The AutoShapes.

The function of most of the Objects Tools are self-evident. They allow you to create various frames and different shapes, including Custom Shapes, as shown in Fig. 12.12, and a selection of Design Objects. For these and other design tools, type their name in the **Search for** box in the **Publisher Help** screen and look up the results.

Creating a Blank Publication

You create a blank publication if you want Publisher to set the dimensions of the publication, but you want to specify your own text and design. To do this, use the **View, Task Pane** command to display the Task Pane, if not visible, then click its down-arrow and select **New Publication**, followed by **Blank Publications** from the drop-down menus, to display what is shown Fig. 12.13 below.

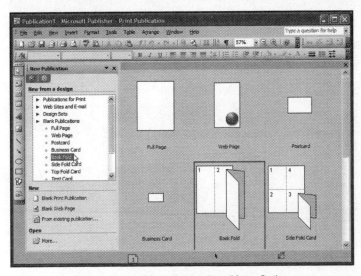

Fig. 12.13 The Blank Publications Menu Option.

As you can see, there are several page set-ups to choose from, including some that require folding. These types of publications print pages on one sheet of paper that can be folded into a booklet.

To illustrate the process, click on the **Book Fold** publication which displays the help box shown in Fig. 12.14 on the next page. This box informs you how many pages are available in the built-in design and asks you whether you would like to add more. As in this case the nature of the chosen design is such that four pages would be preferable to one, it would be a good idea to accept the proposal.

Fig. 12.14 The Insert Pages Help Box.

Clicking the **Yes** button displays the Publisher screen similar to that in Fig. 12.15.

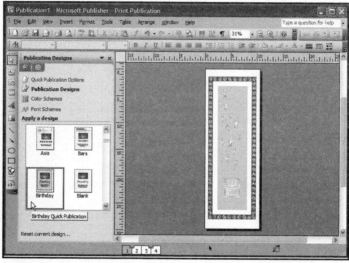

Fig. 12.15 Page Navigation Icons for a Multiple Page Publication.

When you finish creating a blank publication, the program allows you to change its design, colour scheme, and layout, in the same way as when you created a publication using a standard design. In Fig. 12.15 we selected the Birthday Quick Publication design.

If you have more than one page in your publication, Publisher displays page icons at the bottom of the screen, as shown in Fig. 12.15. You can use these icons to navigate through your publication. If you need to add more pages to a publication, use the **Insert, Page** command. Pages can be added before or after the current page using the dialogue box.

Saving your Work

To save your Microsoft Publisher work, use the **File, Save**, or **File, Save As** command which displays the Save As

Fig. 12.16 The Save As Dialogue Box.

dialogue box shown in Fig. 12.16. As usual, we will be saving our work in the **Office 2003 Docs** folder with all the rest of the examples in this book. After locating the folder, save

your design under the filename **Publication 1**. The extension **.pub** is automatically added by the program so that Publisher can distinguish this file as its own. Should you try to exit Publisher without saving your work, the program displays a warning box.

Opening an Existing File

To Open an already saved file when first starting Publisher,

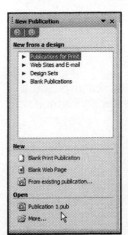

Fig. 12.17 Opening an Existing File.

click its name which displays automatically under the **Open** option at the bottom of the **New Publication** Task Pane, as shown in Fig. 12.17.

If on the other hand you are already working with Publisher and want to open a different file, then click the **Open** button, shown here, on the Standard Toolbar, to display the Open dialogue box, as shown in Fig. 12.18 on the next page.

To open a saved file, navigate to the folder in which you saved your work (ours is the **Office 2003 Docs** folder), and either highlight the required file and click the **Open** button, or simply double-click it.

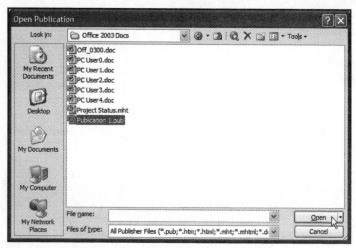

Fig. 12.18 The Open Publication Dialogue Box.

We suggest you open the file **Publication 1**, which we saved earlier, and practise moving its frames, re-sizing them, and adding your own text. Publisher guides you throughout - it couldn't be simpler. Try producing a Birthday Card.

Printing your Work

There are three ways to print and reproduce a publication using Publisher. These printing methods depend on the type of reproduction and quality you require.

- Use a desktop printer for a limited number of copies provided the quality of your printer meets your needs.

- Supply files to a copy shop for a large quantity of copies at an economic cost. The quality will be better than most desktop printers.

- Use a commercial printing service when you want the highest quality printing. For large runs, commercial printing costs can be competitive with copy shops. Using a commercial printing service requires you to take your files with you.

Before you print your work on your desktop printer, make sure that you have an adequate supply of the type and size of paper your publication requires. Then use the **File, Page Setup** command to display the dialogue box shown in Fig. 12.19.

Fig. 12.19 The Page Setup Dialogue Box.

As you can see, depending on the design of your publication, the Page Setup dialogue box reflects the appropriate printing requirements. Make your specific selection and press **OK**, then use the **File, Print** command (or press the **Print** button on the Standard Toolbar), to begin printing. However, before printing your work, don't forget to spell-check it, then preview it.

If you intend to have your publication printed at a copy shop or at a commercial printing service, find out their requirements before you start your design. Apart from the available paper size, you need to know the preferred method of delivering your work; take files on disc, send files via the Internet, or deliver a master copy.

Finally, you could use Publisher to design your very own Web site. Have a look at the **Web Sites** option, to be found under **New Publication**, **Web Sites and E-mail**, category, which activates the Easy Web Site Builder that helps you put together your requirements. To save your creation, use the **File, Save As** command and select 'Web Page' in the **Save as type** box. Be sure to use the **File**, **Web Page Preview** to see your creation as it would appear on your Web site, before using the **File**, **Publish to the Web** command. We leave this to you to try by yourself, as this is beyond the scope of this book.

* * *

Publisher is obviously capable of a lot more than we have introduced here, but you should now be in a position to explore more of the package's facilities by yourself. Try it and have fun!

* * *

13

The Access 2003 Database

Microsoft Access 2003 is a database management system (DBMS) designed to allow users to store, manipulate and retrieve information easily and quickly. A database is a collection of data that exists and is organised around a specific theme or requirement. It can be of the 'flat-file' type, or it can have relational capabilities, as in the case of Access, which is known as a relational database management system (RDBMS).

The main difference between flat-file and relational database systems is that the latter can store and manipulate data in multiple 'tables', while the former systems can only manipulate a single table at any given time. To make accessing the data easier, each row (or **record**) of data within a database table is structured in the same fashion, i.e., each record will have the same number of columns (or **fields**).

We define a database and its various elements as:

Database	A collection of data organised for a specific theme in one or more tables.
Table	A two-dimensional structure in which data is stored, like in a spreadsheet
Record	A row of information in a table relating to a single entry and comprising one or more fields.
Field	A single column of information of the same type, such as people's names.

In Access 2003 the maximum size of a database is 2 gigabytes and in addition it can include linked tables in other files. The number of objects in a database is limited to 32,768, while the maximum number of fields in a table is 255.

A good example of a flat-file database is the invoicing details kept on clients by a company. These details could include name of client, description of work done, invoice number, and amount charged, as shown in Fig. 13.1:

NAME	Consultancy	Invoice	Value
VORTEX Co. Ltd	Wind Tunnel Tests	0401	120.84
AVON Construction	Adhesive Tests	0402	103.52
BARROWS Associates	Tunnel Design Tests	0403	99.32
STONEAGE Ltd	Carbon Dating Tests	0404	55.98
PARKWAY Gravel	Material Size Tests	0405	180.22
WESTWOOD Ltd	Load Bearing Tests	0406	68.52

Fig. 13.1 An Example of a Flat-File Database.

Such a flat-file DBMS is too limited for the type of information normally held by most companies. If the same client asks for work to be carried out regularly, then the details for that client (which could include address, telephone and fax numbers, contact name, date of invoice, etc.), will have to be entered several times. This can lead to errors, but above all to redundant information being kept on a client - each entry will have to have the name of the client, their address, telephone and fax numbers.

The relational facilities offered by Access, overcome the problems of entry errors and duplication of information. The ability to handle multiple tables at any one time allows for the grouping of data into sensible subsets. For example, one table, called client, could hold the names of the clients, their addresses, telephone and fax numbers, while another table, called invoice, could hold information on the work done, invoice number, date of issue, and amount charged. The two tables must have one unique common field, such as a client reference number. The advantage is that details of each client are entered and stored only once, thus reducing the time and effort wasted on entering duplicate information, and also reducing the space required for data storage.

Starting the Access Program

Access is started in Windows either by clicking the **start** button then selecting **All Programs, Microsoft Office** and clicking on the Microsoft Access icon on the cascade menu, or by double-clicking on an Access document file. In the latter case the document will be loaded into Access at the same time.

When you first start Access 2003 the program momentarily displays its opening screen, shown in Fig. 13.2, and then displays the first page of a new document (more about this shortly).

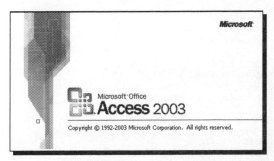

Fig. 13.2 Access' Opening Screen.

Whether you have used a previous version of Access or not, the first time you use the program, it might be a good idea to click the **Microsoft Office Access Help** button on the toolbar, then click the **Table of Contents** link on the **Access Help** Task Pane. This displays a list of help books, and clicking the first one opens a list of help topics as shown in Fig. 13.3 on the next page.

Clicking the 'What's New in Microsoft Access 2003' link, pointed to in Fig. 13.3, opens a separate Help window with a list of additional topics. As you click each hypertext link, Access Help displays several topics on the subject which you might find helpful. We suggest you spend a little time here browsing through the various topics before going on.

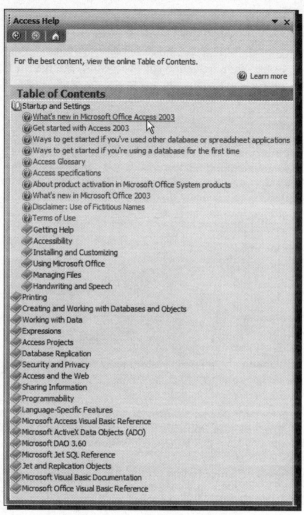

Fig. 13.3 The Microsoft Access Help Screen.

For additional information, click the **Learn more** button on the Access Help, Table of Contents screen, shown in Fig. 13.3 above, which will take you to mainly online topics. However, do investigate the 'Finding templates on your computer' link.

Parts of the Access Screen

Before we start designing a database, let us take a look at the Access opening screen. In Fig. 13.4, we also show what displays if you use **File**, **New**, then at the bottom of the **New File** Task Pane click the **On my computer** link.

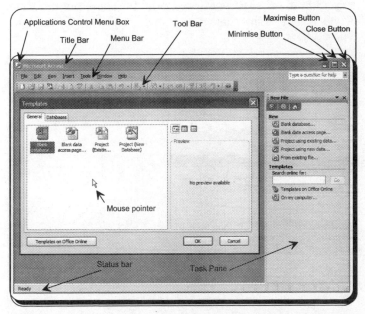

Fig. 13.4 The Access 2003 Opening Screen.

As you can see, these windows have common screen elements with those of other Microsoft Office applications. As usual, depending on what you are doing with Access, the items on the menu bar can be different from those of the opening screen.

Clicking the Databases tab of the Templates box shown in Fig. 13.4 above, displays a list of ready made database templates to suit various tasks, such as 'Asset Tracking', 'Contact Management', 'Event Management', 'Expenses', etc. It is worth having a look at these.

Database Elements

Before we start designing a database using Microsoft Access, it would be a good idea to look at the various elements that make up a database. To do so, start Access and click the **Create New File** link at the bottom of the **Getting Started** Task Pane, which displays the screen in Fig 13.5. If Access is already up and running but the Task Pane is not visible, use the **View, Toolbars, Task Pane** command to open it.

Fig. 13.5 The Access General Templates Dialogue Box.

To create a new database, click the **Blank database** link, pointed to in Fig. 13.5 above, which opens the File New Database dialogue box shown in Fig. 13.6 on the next page.

As usual, we will create our new database in the **Office 2003 Docs** folder which is located in **My Documents**, therefore use the down-arrow against the **Save in** box to navigate to it.

Fig. 13.6 The File New Database Dialogue Box.

In the **File name** box, type the database name, say **Adept 1**, which replaces the default name **db1**. Access adds the extension **.mdb** automatically. Finally, pressing the **Create** button displays the Database dialogue box shown below.

Fig. 13.7 The Database Dialogue Box.

It is from here that you can design the various elements that make up a database, such as Tables, Queries, Forms, and Reports, all of which we will examine in some detail in this and the next chapter.

Creating a Table

To design a database table, select Tables from the **Objects** list and double-click one of the three table-creation buttons displayed on the Database dialogue box. We will choose to use the second button, which opens the Table Wizard with the option of selecting one of two predefined table applications, Business or Personal, as shown in Fig. 13.8.

Fig. 13.8 The Table Wizard Box.

The same dialogue box can be opened by clicking the **New** button on the Database dialogue box which opens the New Table dialogue box shown in Fig. 13.9. The third option starts the Table Wizard, while the penultimate option allows you to import tables and objects from an external file into the current database, and the last option allows you to link a table in the current database to external tables.

Fig. 13.9 The Table Wizard Box.

The database we are going to create holds the invoicing details which the firm Adept Consultants keep on their clients. One table will hold the details of the clients, while another will hold the actual invoice details. Therefore, to start, choose 'Customers' from the **Sample Tables** list of the Table Wizard dialogue box, to reveal a list of appropriate fields for that table, as shown in Fig. 13.10.

Fig. 13.10 Selecting a Table Category from the Table Wizard.

You can either select all the fields or you can select a few. For our example, we selected the following fields: CustomerID, CompanyName, BillingAddress, City, StateOrProvince, PostalCode, ContactTitle, PhoneNumber, FaxNumber and Notes, by highlighting each in turn and pressing the ⯈ button.

Don't worry if these field names are not exactly what you

want, as they can be easily changed. To change field names, highlight them in turn in the 'Fields in my new table' list and click the **Rename Field** button to reveal the Rename field dialogue box shown here.

We suggest you change the selected field names to those listed below.

CustomerID	CustomerID
CompanyName	Name
BillingAddress	Address
City	Town
StateOrProvince	County
PostalCode	PostCode
ContactTitle	Contact
PhoneNumber	Phone
FaxNumber	Fax
Notes	Order

When you have completed renaming the field names, press the **Next** button, which displays the first of two dialogue boxes. In each of these, do the following:

- In answer to the question 'What do you want to name your table?', accept the suggested name **Customers** and press **Next**.

- In answer to the question 'After the wizard creates the table, what do you want to do?', click the **Enter data directly into the table** radio button, and press **Finish**.

This displays the Customers table, as shown in Fig. 13.11 below, ready for you to enter data.

Fig. 13.11 The Customers Table Data Entry Screen.

To redesign the table, including changing its field names, click the **Design View** button shown here, and select the **Design View** option from the drop-down menu, or use the **View**, **Design View** command, to display the Customers Table shown in Fig. 13.12

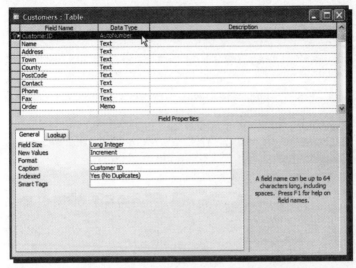

Fig. 13.12 The Customers Table in Design View.

As each field name is highlighted, a Field Properties box appears at the bottom of the screen. If you were using this Table View to rename fields, then you should also edit the name appearing against the Caption property, or remove it altogether.

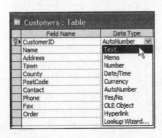

Next, place the cursor at the end of the Data Type descriptor of the CustomerID field which causes a down-arrow button to be displayed. Clicking this, displays a list of data types, as shown here in Fig. 13.13.

Fig. 13.13 The List of Data Types.

As we will be using text to give our customers a unique ID, change the data type of this field from **AutoNumber** to **Text**.

Having done so, click the **Save** button (or use the **File, Save** command) to save your design changes up to this point. Next, as the Order field was renamed from one called Notes, Access expects entries in this field to be of Memo type by default. However, we intend to use this field as an auto-numbering field, keeping track of the order in which records were added to the database. Hence, we must change the current data type to AutoNumber and re-save our changes. It is important to do the intermediate save, because Access does not allow the removal of an AutoNumber field at the same time as changing another field to this type.

Finally, click the **Datasheet View** button (or use the **View, Datasheet View** command) to revert to the Customers table so that you can start entering information, as shown in Fig. 13.14. The required data for the rest of the fields is shown in Fig. 13.16 on the next page.

Customer ID	Name	Address	Town	County	Post Code
VORT	VORTEX Co. Ltd	Windy House	St. Austell	Cornwall	TR18 1FX
AVON	AVON Construction	Riverside House	Stratford-on-Avon	Warwickshire	AV15 2QW
BARR	BARROWS Associates	Barrows House	Bodmin	Cornwall	PL22 1XE
STON	STONEAGE Ltd	Data House	Salisbury	Wiltshire	SB44 1BN
PARK	PARKWAY Gravel	Aggregate House	Bristol	Avon	BS55 2ZX
WEST	WESTWOOD Ltd	Weight House	Plymouth	Devon	PL22 1AA
GLOW	GLOWORM Ltd	Light House	Brighton	Sussex	BR87 4DD
SILV	SILVERSMITH Co	Radiation House	Exeter	Devon	EX28 1PL
WORM	WORMGLAZE Ltd	Glass House	Winchester	Hampshire	WN23 5TR
EALI	EALING Engines Design	Engine House	Taunton	Somerset	TN17 3RT
HIRE	HIRE Service Equipment	Network House	Bath	Avon	BA76 3WE
EURO	EUROBASE Co. Ltd	Control House	Penzance	Cornwall	TR15 8LK

Fig. 13.14 Data Entered in Customers Table of Database.

The widths of the above fields were changed so that all fields

Customer ID	Name
VORT	VORTEX Co. Ltd
AVON	AVON Construction
BARR	BARROWS Associates
STON	STONEAGE Ltd

Fig. 13.15 Changing the Column Width.

could be visible on the screen at the same time. To change the width of a field, place the cursor on the column separator until the cursor changes to the vertical split arrow, as shown in Fig. 13.15, then drag the column separator to the right or left, to increase or decrease the width of the field.

Sorting a Database Table

As you enter information into a database table, you might elect to change the field headings by clicking the **Design View** button and editing a field name, say from Name to CompanyName. If you do this, on return to the Customers table you will find that the records have sorted automatically in ascending order of the entries of the field in which you left the cursor while in the Design Table.

Contact	Phone	Fax	Order
Brian Storm	01776-223344	01776-224466	1
John Waters	01657-113355	01657-221133	2
Mandy Brown	01554-664422	01554-663311	3
Mike Irons	01765-234567	01765-232332	4
James Stone	01534-987654	01534-984567	5
Mary Slim	01234-667755	01234-669988	6
Peter Summers	01432-746523	01432-742266	7
Adam Smith	01336-997755	01336-996644	8
Richard Glazer	01123-654321	01123-651234	9
Trevor Miles	01336-010107	01336-010109	10
Nicole Webb	01875-558822	01875-552288	11
Sarah Star	01736-098765	01736-098567	12
			(AutoNumber)

Fig. 13.16 Additional Data for Customers Table.

If you want to preserve the order in which you entered your data, then sort by the last field (Order) with its type as AutoNumber. This can be done at any time, even after you have finished entering all other information in your table.

Sorting a database table in ascending order of an AutoNumber type field, results in the database table displaying in the order in which the data was originally entered in that table. Above, we show the Contact field, so that you can cross-check the original order of your Customer table, as well as the rest of the information in that table not shown in the screen dump of the previous page.

To sort a database table in ascending or descending order of the entries of any field, place the cursor in the required field and click the **Sort Ascending** or **Sort Descending** button, shown here. To see these toolbar buttons, you must be in **Datasheet View**.

To sort records using menu commands, click the **Records, Sort** command, then select either the **Sort Ascending** or the **Sort Descending** option.

Applying a Filter to a Sort

If you would like to sort and display only records that fit selected criteria, use the **Records, Filter, Advanced Filter/Sort** command, which opens the Filter dialogue box, shown in Fig. 13.17.

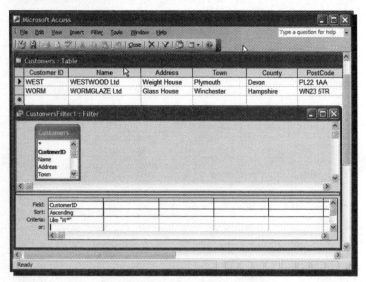

Fig. 13.17 Applying a Filter to a Sort.

The upper portion of the dialogue box displays all the fields in the Customers table, while the lower portion is where you enter your filter restrictions. In the above example, we chose to view, in ascending order, the records within the CustomerID field that start with W - we typed W* and when we moved to the next field, Access displayed it as *Like "W*"*.

On pressing the **Apply Filter** button on the Standard Toolbar, shown here, the Customers table displays with only two entries, as seen in the above composite screen dump in which the filter restrictions as well as the result arising from such a filter are displayed. To revert to the display of all the records, click the same button again, which now appears on the Toolbar depressed, and bears the name **Remove Filter**. You might have to sort the data by ascending 'Order' to get them back as they were before.

Using a Database Form

Once a table has been selected from the Database window,

clicking the down-arrow against the **New Object** button and selecting **AutoForm**, automatically displays each record of that table in form view. The created form for the Customers table is shown in Fig. 13.18. Before the Form View object is created you will be asked whether to save your Customers table, as it depends on it.

Forms can be used to enter, change or view data. They are mainly used to improve the way in which data is displayed on the screen.

Forms can also be used to sort records in a database table in descending or ascending order of a selected field.

Fig. 13.18 An AutoForm for Customers Table.

When you attempt to close a new **Form** window, you will be asked if you would like to save it. An Access database can have lots of different forms, each designed with a different purpose in mind. Saved forms are displayed in the Database window when you click the **Forms** button in the Objects menu. In the above example, we chose the default name suggested by Access, which was Customers.

In the next chapter we will discuss Form design in some detail, including their customisation.

Working with Data

Adding Records to a Table: Whether you are in Table view or Form view, to add a record, click the **New Record** button, shown here.

When in Table view, the cursor jumps to the first empty record in the table (the one with the asterisk in the box to the left of the first field). When in Form view, Access displays an empty form which can be used to add a new record.

Finding Records in a Table: Whether you are in Table or Form view, to find a record click the **Find** button, or use **Edit, Find** to open the dialogue box shown in Fig 13.19.

Fig. 13.19 Finding Records in a Table.

Note the field name in the **Look In** box of the dialogue box, which is CustomerID, indicating that we are only interested in finding a match within the CustomerID field.

To find all the records starting with **w**, we type **w*** in the **Find What** box of the dialogue box. Pressing the **Find Next** button, highlights the first record with the CustomerID 'WEST'. Pressing the **Find Next** button again, highlights the next record that matches our selected criteria, which in this case will be 'WORM'.

Deleting Records from a Table: To delete a record when in
Table view, point to the box to the left of the record to
highlight the entire record, as shown in Fig. 13.20 below, then
either click the **Delete Record** toolbar button, shown
here, or press the <Del> key.

| HIRE | HIRE Service Equipment | Network House | Bath | Avon | BA76 3WE |
| EURO | EUROBASE Co. Ltd | Control House | Penzance | Cornwall | TR15 8LK |

Fig. 13.20 Selecting a Record for Deletion.

To delete a record when in Form view, first display the record
you want to delete, then use the **Edit, Select Record**
command to select the whole record, and press the <Del>
key.

In both cases you will be given a warning and you will be
asked to confirm your decision. However, linked records
(more about this shortly), cannot be deleted.

Delete, Insert, and Move Fields in a Table: To delete a
field from a table, close any forms that might be
open, load the table from the Database window,
then click the **Design View** button, click the row
selector to highlight the field you want to remove, as
shown in Fig. 13.21 below, and click the **Delete
Rows** button, shown here, or use the **Edit, Delete**
command.

Field Name	Data Type	
CustomerID	Text	
Name	Text	
Address	Text	
Town	Text	
County	Text	

Fig. 13.21 Selecting a Field for Deletion.

To insert a field in a table, display the table in Design View,
and highlight the field above which you want to insert the new
field, and click the **Insert Rows** button, shown here, or
use the **Insert, Rows** command.

To move a field from its current to a new position in a table, select the field you want to move in Design View, then point to the row selector so that the mouse pointer is inclined as shown in Fig. 13.22, and drag the row to its new position.

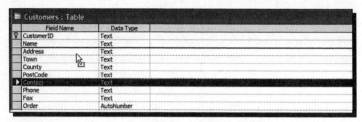

Fig. 13.22 Moving a Field in a Table.

Note that while you are dragging the field, the mouse pointer changes to the one pointing at the Name field in the above composite. Releasing the mouse button, moves the Contact field to the position of the thin horizontal line and pushes all other fields below it one row down.

Printing a Table View

You can print a database table by clicking the **Print** button, or by using the **File, Print** command which displays the Print dialogue box shown in Fig. 13.23. Alternatively, you can preview a database on screen by clicking the **Preview** button.

Fig. 13.23 The Print Dialogue Box.

However, printing directly from here, produces a predefined printout, the format of which you cannot control, apart from the margins and print orientation. To control these, click the **Setup** or **Properties** button.

For a better method of producing a printed output, see the Report Design section in the next chapter.

Relational Database Design

In order to be able to discuss relational databases, we will add an Orders table to our database by doing the following:

- Open the **Adept 1** database and with the Tables Object active, click the **New** Toolbar button.

- Use the Table Wizard and select 'Orders' from the displayed **Sample Tables** list. Next, select the five fields displayed below under **Fields in my new table** from the **Sample Fields** list, and press **Next**.

Fig. 13.24 Creating an Orders Table for Adept 1 Database.

In the next four dialogue boxes, do the following:

- Accept the default name (Orders), click the **No, I'll set the primary key** radio button, and press **Next**.

- Accept the default field (OrderID) as the field which holds data that is unique to each record, click the **Numbers and/or letters I enter when I add new records** radio button and press **Next**.

- On the next dialogue box you specify whether the new table is related to any other tables in the database. Accept the default which is, that it is not related, and press **Next**.

Although the two tables are actually related, we chose at this stage to tell the Wizard that they are not. This might appear to you as odd, but the Wizard makes certain assumptions about unique fields (for example, that ID fields are numbers), which is not what we want them to be. We choose to remain in control of the design of our database and, therefore, we will define the relationship between the two tables later.

* In the final dialogue box, click the **Enter data directly into the table** radio button, and press **Finish**.

The Wizard displays the newly created table ready for you to enter your data. However, before doing so, use the Design Table facility, as discussed previously, to change the Data Types of the selected Field Names to those displayed here. Also, change the length of the first field (OrderID) from 4 to 8 characters.

Fig. 13.25 Changing Data Types.

The information you need to enter in the Orders table is shown in Fig. 13.26 below.

Order ID	Customer ID	Employee ID	Order Date	Ship Date
04002STO	STON	C. H. Wills	06/01/2004	12/01/2004
04006PAR	PARK	A. D. Smith	02/02/2004	13/02/2004
04010WES	WEST	W. A. Brown	26/02/2004	05/03/2004
04018GLO	GLOW	L. S. Stevens	26/03/2004	08/04/2004
04025SIL	SILV	S. F. Adams	29/04/2004	10/05/2004
04029WOR	WORM	C. H. Wills	01/06/2004	11/06/2004
04039EAL	EALI	A. D. Smith	02/07/2004	13/07/2004
04045HIR	HIRE	W. A. Brown	12/08/2004	23/08/2004
04051EUR	EURO	L. S. Stevens	09/09/2004	17/09/2004
04064AVO	AVON	S. F. Adams	30/09/2004	12/10/2004
04085VOR	VORT	A. D. Smith	28/10/2004	05/11/2004
04097AVO	AVON	W. A. Brown	25/11/2004	01/12/2004
04099BAR	BARR	S. F. Adams	13/12/2004	20/12/2004

Record: 13 of 13

Fig. 13.26 Data for the Orders Table.

Relationships

Information held in two or more tables of a database is normally related in some way. In our case, the two tables, Customers and Orders, are related by the CustomerID field.

To build up relationships between tables, return to the Database window and click the **Relationships** button on the Tool bar, shown here. This opens the Show Table dialogue box in which you select each table in turn and click the **Add** button. This places the tables in the Relationships window with the index field in each table shown emboldened.

You can build relationships between tables by dragging a field name from one table into another. In our example (Fig. 13.27), we have dragged the CustomerID field from the Customers table (by pointing to it, pressing the left mouse button, and while keeping the mouse button pressed, dragging the pointer) to the required field in the other table, in this case CustomerID in the Orders table.

Fig. 13.27 Building Relationships Between Tables.

Releasing the mouse button opens the dialogue boxes shown in Fig. 13.28 on the next page (the **Join Properties** dialogue box is displayed by pressing the **Join Type** button on the Edit Relationships dialogue box).

Fig. 13.28 Specifying the Type of Join in New Queries.

In the Join Properties dialogue box you can specify the type of join Access should create in new queries - more about this later. For the present, press the **OK** button on the Join Properties dialogue box, to close it, then check the **Enforce Referential Integrity** box in the Relationships dialogue box, and press the **Create** button.

Access creates and displays graphically the chosen type of relationship in the Relationships window shown in Fig. 13.29. Note the relationship '1 customer to many (∞) orders' symbolism in the Relationships window.

Because Access is a relational database, data can be used in queries from more than one table at a time. As

Fig. 13.29 The Relationships Screen.

we have seen, if the database contains tables with related data, the relationships can be defined easily.

Usually, the matching fields have the same name, as in our example of Customers and Orders tables. In the Customers table, the CustomerID field is the primary field and relates to the CustomerID field in the Orders table - there can be several orders in the Orders table from one customer in the Customers table.

The various types of relationships are as follows:

* Inherited - for attaching tables from another Access database. The original relationships of the attached database can be used in the current database.

* Referential - for enforcing relationships between records according to certain rules, when you add or delete records in related tables within the same database. For example, you can only add records to a related table, if a matching record already exists in the primary table, and you cannot delete a record from the primary table if matching records exist in a related table, as we mentioned earlier.

Viewing and Editing Relationships

To view the current relationships between tables, activate the Database window and press the **Relationships** button.

To edit a relationship, double-click the left mouse button at the pointer position shown here. The tip of the mouse pointer must be on the inclined line joining the two tables in the Relationships window, as shown, before Access will respond. If you have difficulty with this action, first point to the relationship line and click once to embolden it, then use the **Relationships, Edit Relationship** command. Either of these two actions will open the Relationships dialogue box in which you can change the various options already discussed.

To remove a relationship, activate it (point and click to embolden it), then press the <Del> key. To delete a table, you must first detach it from other tables, then select it in the Database Window and press the <Del> key.

Creating an Additional Table

As an exercise, create a third table using the Table Wizard and select Invoices from the displayed **Sample Tables** list. Then choose the five fields displayed below - the names and their data types have been changed using the Design Table facility. Also in Fig. 13.30 we have included instructions under 'Description' relating to field lengths and default values for you to apply to the Field Properties box of each Data Type.

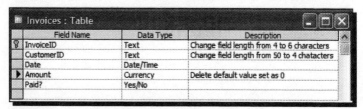

Field Name	Data Type	Description
InvoiceID	Text	Change field length from 4 to 6 characters
CustomerID	Text	Change field length from 50 to 4 chatacters
Date	Date/Time	
Amount	Currency	Delete default value set as 0
Paid?	Yes/No	

Fig. 13.30 Creating an Invoices Table.

Next, enter the data given below and build up appropriate relationships between the Invoices table, the Customers table and the Orders table, as shown on the next page.

Invoice ID	Customer ID	Date	Amount	Paid?
AD0101	STON	12/01/2004	£55.98	☐
AD0102	PARK	13/02/2004	£180.22	☐
AD0103	WEST	05/03/2004	£68.52	☐
AD0104	GLOW	08/04/2004	£111.56	☐
AD0105	SILV	10/05/2004	£123.45	☑
AD0106	WORM	11/06/2004	£35.87	☐
AD0107	EALI	13/07/2004	£58.95	☐
AD0108	HIRE	23/08/2004	£290.00	☐
AD0109	EURO	17/09/2004	£150.00	☐
AD0110	AVON	12/10/2004	£103.52	☑
AD0111	VORT	05/11/2004	£120.84	☐
AD0112	AVON	01/12/2004	£135.00	☐
AD0113	BARR	20/12/2004	£99.32	☐

Record: 1 of 13

Fig. 13.31 Data for Invoices Table of Adept 1 Database.

The relationships between the three tables should be arranged as follows:

Fig. 13.32 The Relationships Between Tables.

It is important that you should complete this exercise, as it consolidates what we have done so far and, in any case, we will be using all three tables in what comes next. So go ahead and try it, the resultant database will be saved automatically under its original filename **Adept 1**.

14

Forms, Reports & Queries

In this chapter, we introduce the subject of Forms, Reports, and Queries. We will show you how to use the various Wizards to create:

- Forms to find, edit, and add data in a convenient manner. Access provides you with an easy way of designing various types of forms, some of which are discussed here. Forms look good on screen, but do not produce very good output on paper.

- Reports to produce good looking output on paper. However, reports do not necessarily look good on screen.

- Queries so that you can ask questions about the data in your database tables. For example, we could find out whether we have more than one order from the same customer in our Adept database.

Creating Forms

We saw in the previous chapter how easy it was to create a single column form to view our Customers table. To see this again, open **Adept 1** and in the Database window click the **Forms** button in the **Objects** list, as shown in Fig. 14.1, then double-click the Customers entry.

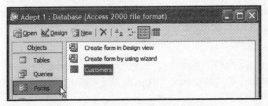

Fig. 14.1 Creating a Single Column Form.

Using the Form Wizard

You can use the Form Wizard to easily display data from either a table or a query in form view.

In the Database window, first click the **Forms** button in the **Objects** list, then the **New** button on the Toolbar, which opens the New Form dialogue box, shown below. As you can see from this screen dump, there are different types of forms available for you to choose from. Their function will be discussed shortly.

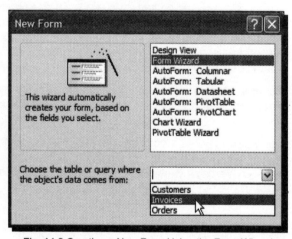

Fig. 14.2 Creating a New Form Using the Form Wizard.

To continue with our example, we first selected the Form Wizard, then chose the Invoices table on which to base the new form, and pressed the **OK** button (which is obscured in the above screen dump by the drop-down list of database tables). This causes the Wizard to display the first of four additional dialogue boxes, shown on the next page, in which you are asked to specify the fields that contain the data you want to include. We chose all the fields.

As usual, after making appropriate selections, click the **Next** button to progress through the automatic design of the particular form.

Fig. 14.3 Selecting the Fields for the New Form.

In the next three dialogue boxes that are displayed by the Wizard, make the following selections in order of appearance:

- **Columnar** for the layout of your form.
- **Standard** as the style for your Labels and Data.
- **Open the form to view or enter information**.

Pressing the **Finish** button, displays the following form.

Fig. 14.4 The New Invoices Form.

Types of Forms

The available choice of Form designs have the function shown in the table below.

Type of Form	Function
Design View	Design a form from scratch.
Form Wizard	Automatically creates a form based on the fields you select.
AutoForm: Columnar	Creates a columnar form with all the field labels appearing in the first column and the data in the second. The form displays one record at a time.
AutoForm: Tabular	Tabulates a screen full of records in tabular form with the field labels appearing at the head of each column.
AutoForm: Datasheet	Similar to the Tabular form, but in worksheet display format.
Chart Wizard	Displays data graphically.
PivotTable Wizard	Creates a form with an Excel PivotTable - an interactive table that can summarise a large number of data using the format and calculation methods specified by the user.

Access also allows you to design a form that contains another form. This type of form, called main/subform, allows data from related tables to be viewed at the same time.

Subforms are especially effective when you want to show data from tables or queries with a one-to-many relationship. For example, you could create a form with a subform to show data from a Customers table and an Invoices table. The data in the Customers table is the 'one' side of the relationship, while the data in the invoices table is the 'many' side of the relationship - each customer can be issued with more than one invoice.

Customising a Form

You can customise a form by changing the appearance of text, data, and any other attributes. To have a look at some of these options, double-click on Customers to display the Customers form, then click the **Design View** button on the Toolbar.

What appears on your screen when the Toolbox button is activated is shown in Fig. 14.5 .

Fig. 14.5 The Customers Form in Design View.

As you can see, a form in Design View is made up of label and data boxes. Clicking at the County box, for example, causes markers to appear around it as shown above. When the mouse pointer is then placed within either the label box or data box, it changes to a hand (as shown), which indicates that you can drag the box to a new position, as we have done above. This method moves both label and data boxes together.

If you look more closely at the markers around the label and data boxes, you will see that they are of different size, as shown below.

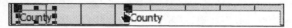

Fig. 14.6 Label and Data Markers.

The larger ones are 'move' handles, while the smaller ones are 'size' handles. In the above example you can use the 'move' handles on either the label or the data box (as shown) to move one independently of the other. Note the shape of the hand in this case which is different to our previous screen dump.

The label box can also be sized. To size the data box, click on it so that the markers appear around it. Boxes on a form can be made larger by simply pointing to the sizing handles and dragging them in the appropriate direction.

In addition to moving and enlarging label and data boxes, you can further customise a form using the various buttons that appear on the Formatting Toolbar when in Design or Form View, shown below in Fig. 14.7.

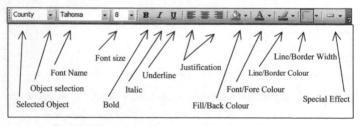

Fig. 14.7 Toolbar Buttons when in Design or Form View.

Do try and experiment with moving and sizing label and data boxes and also increasing their font size. If you don't like the result, simply don't save it. Skills gained here will be used in the Report design section.

The Toolbox

The Toolbox can be used either to design a Form or Report from scratch (a task beyond the scope of this book), or to add controls to them, such as a Combo (drop-down) box. The function of each tool on the Toolbox is listed below.

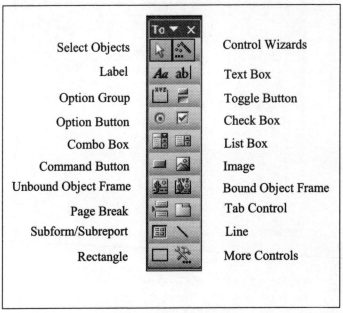

Select Objects			Control Wizards
Label			Text Box
Option Group			Toggle Button
Option Button			Check Box
Combo Box			List Box
Command Button			Image
Unbound Object Frame			Bound Object Frame
Page Break			Tab Control
Subform/Subreport			Line
Rectangle			More Controls

Fig. 14.8 The Toolbox Buttons.

As an example of using the Toolbox, let us assume that we would like to use a form to enter new data into our Invoices table, but with the ability of selecting the CustomerID field from a drop-down menu - a Combo box.

To achieve this, execute the following steps:

- On the Database window first click the **Forms** button in the **Objects** list, then double-click on Invoices. If you have not created the Invoice form, you must do so as explained in the 'Using the Form Wizard' section at the beginning of this chapter, before going on.

- When the Invoice form appears on the screen, click the **Design View** button on the Toolbar, and enlarge the Invoices form so that both the Header and Footer sections are visible on the form, as shown in Fig. 14.9.

Fig. 14.9 The Invoices Form in Design View.

- Click the CustomerID field on the form, and delete both its Label and Data boxes by clicking each individually and pressing the <Del> key.

- Click the Combo Box on the Toolbox, and point and click at the area where the CustomerID data box used to be on the form.

- In the subsequent dialogue boxes, select options which will cause the Combo Box to: (a) look up the values from the Customers table, and from the CustomerID field, (b) sort into ascending order of the Customers table, (c) size the width of the data field, (d) store a selected value in the CustomerID field, and (e) specify that the Combo Box should have the label Customer ID:, before clicking the **Finish** button.

- Move and size both the Label and Data boxes of the Combo box into the position shown in Fig. 14.10.

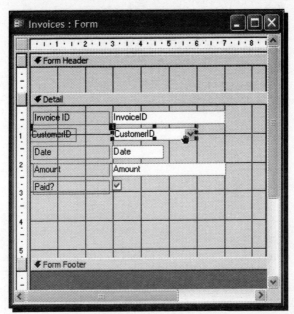

Fig. 14.10 Creating a Combo Box.

- Click the **Form View** button on the Toolbar, followed by the **New Record** button at the bottom of the Invoices form, both of which are shown here to the right.

The entry form should now look as shown in Fig. 14.11 on the next page.

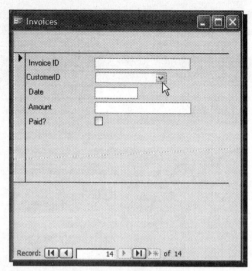

Fig. 14.11 The Invoices Form with a Combo Box.

From now on, whenever you want to add a new invoice to the Invoices table, use the Invoices form from the Database window, then click the **New Record** button on either the Toolbar or the Invoices form itself to display an empty form.

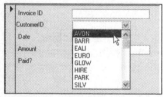

Fig. 14.12 The Customer ID
Combo Box.

Next, type in the relevant information in the appropriate data boxes on the form, but when you come to fill in the Customer ID field, click instead the down arrow against its data box to display the drop-down menu shown in Fig. 14.12. Select one of the existing customers on the list, and click the **Next Record** button ▶ at the bottom of the Invoices form.

Try the above procedure with the following details:

```
AD0114     WEST     21/12/04     £140
```

then verify that indeed the information has been recorded by double-clicking the Invoices table on the Database window. Don't forget to save the changes to the Invoices form.

Using the Report Wizard

We will use the skills gained in manipulating Forms in Design View to produce an acceptable report created by the Report Wizard. To produce a report of the Invoices table, do the following:

- Click the **Reports** button in the **Objects** list on the Database window and then press the **New** button.

- In the New Report dialogue box, select the **Report Wizard** option, and choose 'Invoices' as the table where the object's data will come from, and press **OK**.

- Select all the fields which are to appear on your report and click the **Next** button.

- Select the InvoiceID field as the Grouping level, then choose the Date field as the sort field, and accept all subsequent default settings, but for the Layout select **Block**. Call the report 'Invoices'. The report is created for you, shown in Fig. 14.13 below in its raw state.

CustomerID	InvoiceID	Date	Amount	Paid?
AVON	AD0101	12/01/2004	£55.98	
	AD0110	12/10/2004	£103.52	☑
	AD0112	01/12/2004	£135.00	
BARR	AD0113	20/12/2004	£99.32	
EALI	AD0107	13/07/2004	£58.95	
EURO	AD0109	17/09/2004	£150.00	
GLOW	AD0104	08/04/2004	£111.56	
HIRE	AD0108	23/08/2004	£290.00	
PARK	AD0102	13/02/2004	£180.22	
SILV	AD0105	10/05/2004	£123.45	☑
VORT	AD0111	05/11/2004	£120.84	
WEST	AD0103	05/03/2004	£68.52	
	AD0114	21/12/2004	£140.00	
WORM	AD0106	11/06/2004	£35.87	

Invoices

21 December 2003   *Page 1 of 1*

Fig. 14.13 The Invoices Report.

Creating a Query

You create a query so that you can ask questions about the data in your database tables. For example, we could find out whether we have more than one order from the same customer in our Adept database.

To do this, start Access, open **Adept 1**, and in the Database window click the **Queries** button in the **Objects** list, followed by the **New** button which opens the New Query dialogue box. Selecting the **Find Duplicates Query Wizard**, displays the screen in Fig. 14.14.

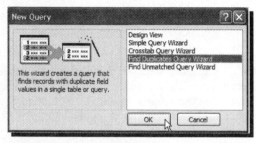

Fig. 14.14 Using the Find Duplicate Query Wizard.

On clicking **OK**, the Find Duplicates Query Wizard dialogue box is displayed, as shown in Fig. 14.15 (you might need to install this feature). Next, select the Orders table from the displayed database tables and press the **Next** button.

Fig. 14.15 Selecting a Table for the Query.

On the following dialogue box select **CustomerID** as the field you want to check for duplicate values, then press the ⮞ button, followed by the **Next** button.

Fig. 14.16 Selecting a Field for the Query.

Finally, select the additional fields you would like to see along with the duplicate values, by selecting those you want from the next dialogue box, either one at a time or, if you decide to select all of them, as shown here, by clicking the ⮞⮞ button.

Fig. 14.17 Selecting Additional Fields for Query.

Clicking the **Finish** button displays the screen in Fig. 14.18.

Customer ID	Order ID	Employee ID	Order Date	Ship Date
AVON	04097AVO	W. A. Brown	25/11/2004	01/12/20
AVON	04064AVO	S. F. Adams	30/09/2004	12/10/20

Record: [◀] [◀] [1] [▶] [▶▮] [▶*] of 2

Fig. 14.18 The Select Query Screen.

Types of Queries

The query we have created so far, is known as a *Select Query*, which is the most common type of query. However, with Access you can also create and use other types of queries, as follows:

- **Crosstab query** - used to present data with row and column headings, just like a spreadsheet. It can be used to summarise large amounts of data in a more readable form.

- **Action query** - used to make changes to many records in one operation. For example, you might like to remove from a given table all records that meet certain criteria, make a new table, or append records to a table. Obviously, this type of query has to be treated with care!

- **Union query** - used to match fields from two or more tables.

- **Pass-through query** - used to pass commands to a SQL (see below) database.

- **Data-definition query** - used to create, change, or delete tables in an Access database using SQL statements.

SQL stands for Structured Query Language, often used to query, update, and manage relational databases. Each query created by Access has an associated SQL statement that defines the action of that query. Thus, if you are familiar with SQL, you can use such statements to view and modify queries, or set form and report properties. However, these actions can be done more easily with the QBE (query-by-example) grid, to be discussed next. If you design union queries, pass-through queries, or data-definition queries, then you must use SQL statements, as these types of queries can not be designed with the QBE grid. Finally, to create a sub-query, you use the QBE grid, but you enter a SQL SELECT statement for criteria, as we shall see in the next QBE grid example.

The Query Window

The Query window is a graphical query-by-example (QBE) tool. Because of Access' graphical features, you can use the mouse to select, drag, and manipulate objects in the query window to define how you would like to see your data.

An example of a ready made Query window can be seen by selecting the Find duplicates for Orders query and clicking the **Design** button on the Database window. This action opens the Select Query dialogue box shown in Fig. 14.19.

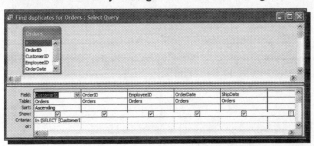

Fig. 14.19 The Select Query Dialogue Box.

You can add a table to the top half of the Query window by dragging the table from the Database window. Similarly, you can add fields to the bottom half of the Query window (the QBE grid) by dragging fields from the tables on the top half of the Query window. Also, the QBE grid is used to select the data sort order, or insert criteria, such as SQL statements.

To see the full SQL SELECT statement written by Access as the criteria selection when we first defined the query, use the **View, SQL View** command.

```
SELECT Orders.CustomerID, Orders.OrderID, Orders.EmployeeID, Orders.OrderDate, Orders.ShipDate
FROM Orders
WHERE (((Orders.CustomerID) In (SELECT [CustomerID] FROM [Orders] As Tmp GROUP BY [CustomerID] HAVING Count(*)>1 )))
ORDER BY Orders.CustomerID;
```

Note the part of the statement which states 'As Tmp GROUP'. Access collects the data you want as a temporary group, called a *dynaset*. This special set of data behaves like a table, but is not a table; it is a dynamic view of the data from one or more tables, selected and sorted by the particular query.

Adding Tables to a Query Window

Below, we show a screen dump created by first clicking the **Queries** button in the **Objects** list, then pressing the **New** button on the Database window. In the displayed New Query dialogue box, select Design View, as shown in Fig. 14.20, and press the **OK** button.

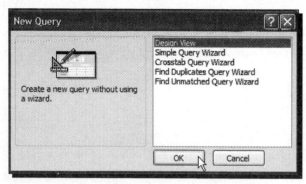

Fig. 14.20 The New Query Dialogue Box.

This opens both the Select Query and the Show Table dialogue boxes shown below. The Invoices and Customers tables were then added to the Select Query window by selecting them in the Show Table dialogue box and pressing the **Add** button, as shown in Fig. 14.21.

Fig. 14.21 The Select Query and Show Table Dialogue Boxes.

Adding Fields to a Query Window

In Fig. 14.22 we show a screen in which the Paid?, InvoiceID, and Amount fields have been dragged from the Invoices table and added to the Query window. Also, the Name and Contact fields have been dragged from the Customers table and placed on the Query window, while the Phone field from the Customers table is about to be added to the Query window.

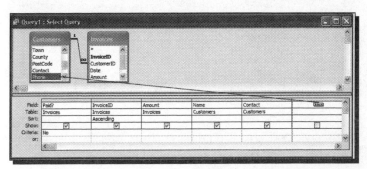

Fig. 14.22 Dragging Fields from Tables to the QBE Grid.

Having dragged all five fields from the two tables onto the QBE grid, we have added the word **No** as the criteria on the Paid? field and selected Ascending as the Sort for the InvoiceID field.

Note that the Invoices and Customers tables are joined by a line that connects the two CustomerID fields. The join line was created when we designed the tables and their relationships in the previous chapter. Even if you have not created these relationships, Access will join the tables in a query automatically when the tables are added to a query, provided each table has a field with the same name and a compatible data type and one of those fields is a primary key. A primary field is displayed in bold in the Query window.

If you have not created relationships between your tables yourself, or Access has not joined your tables automatically, you can still use related data in your query by joining the tables in the Query window.

Clicking the **Run** button on the Toolbar, shown here, instantly displays all the unpaid invoices with the details you have asked for, as follows:

	Paid?	Invoice ID	Amount	Name	Contact	Phone
▶	☐	AD0101	£55.98	AVON Construction	John Waters	01657-113355
	☐	AD0102	£180.22	PARKWAY Gravel	James Stone	01534-987654
	☐	AD0103	£68.52	WESTWOOD Ltd	Mary Slim	01234-667755
	☐	AD0104	£111.56	GLOWORM Ltd	Peter Summers	01432-746523
	☐	AD0106	£35.87	WORMGLAZE Ltd	Richard Glazer	01123-654321
	☐	AD0107	£58.95	EALING Engines Design	Trevor Miles	01336-010107
	☐	AD0108	£290.00	HIRF Service Equipment	Nicole Webb	01875-558822
	☐	AD0109	£150.00	EUROBASE Co. Ltd	Sarah Star	01736-098765
	☐	AD0111	£120.84	VORTEX Co. Ltd	Brian Storm	01776-223344
	☐	AD0112	£135.00	AVON Construction	John Waters	01657-113355
	☐	AD0113	£99.32	BARROWS Associates	Mandy Brown	01554-664422
	☐	AD0114	£140.00	WESTWOOD Ltd	Mary Slim	01234-667755
✱	☐					

Record: |◄| ◄ | 1 | ► | ►| | ►✱ | of 12

Fig. 14.23 Unpaid Invoices from the Adept 1 Database.

To save your newly created query, use the **File, Save As** command, and give it a name such as 'Unpaid Invoices' in the Save As dialogue box.

Types of Criteria

Access accepts the following expressions as criteria:

Arithmetic Operators		Comparison Operators		Logical Operators	
*	Multiply	<	Less than	And	And
/	Divide	<=	Less than or equal	Or	Inclusive or
+	Add	>	Greater than	Xor	Exclusive or
-	Subtract	>=	Greater than or equal	Not	Not equivalent
		=	Equal	Eqv	Equivalent
		<>	Not equal	Imp	Implication
Other operators					
Between	Between 50 And 150	All values between 50 and 150			
In	In ("Bath","Bristol")	All records with Bath and Bristol			
Is	Is Null	All records with no value in that field			
Like	Like "Brian *"	All records with Brian something in field			
&	[Name]&" "&[Surname]	Concatenates strings			

Using Wildcard Characters in Criteria

In a previous example we used the criteria A* to mean any company whose name starts with the letter A. The asterisk in this criteria is known as a wildcard character.

To search for a pattern, you can use the asterisk (*) and the question mark (?) as wildcard characters when specifying criteria in expressions. An asterisk stands for any number of characters, while a question mark stands for any single character in the same position as the question mark.

The following examples show the use of wildcard characters in various types of expressions. However, in a database field all words in that field are considered as an entity. Hence, if you were looking for all occurrences of Mary in, say, the Contact field, you should enter the criteria as Mary*. The asterisk indicates that there is more in that field.

Entered Expression	Meaning	Examples
a?	Any two-letter word beginning with A	am, an, as, at
???d	Any four-letter word ending with d	find, hand, land, yard
Sm?th	Any five-letter word beginning with Sm and ending with th	Smith, Smyth
fie*	Any word starting with the letters fie	field, fiend, fierce, fiery
*ght	Any word ending with ght	alight, eight, fight, light, might, sight
*/5/2004	All dates in May 2004	1/5/2004
a	Any word with the letter a in it	Brian, Mary, star, yard

Combining Criteria

By specifying additional criteria in a Query window you can create powerful queries for viewing your data. In the examples below we have added the field Amount to our Unpaid Invoices query.

The AND Criteria with Different Fields: When you insert criteria in several fields, but in the same row, Access assumes that you are searching for records that meet all of the criteria. For example, the criteria below lists the records shown in Fig. 14.24.

Field:	Paid?	InvoiceID	Amount	Name	Contact
Table:	Invoices	Invoices	Invoices	Customers	Customers
Sort:		Ascending			
Show:	✓	✓	✓	✓	✓
Criteria:	No		Between 50 And 100		
or:					

Paid?	Invoice ID	Amount	Name	Contact	Phone
☐	AD0101	£55.98	AVON Construction	John Waters	01657-113355
☐	AD0103	£68.52	WESTWOOD Ltd	Mary Slim	01234-667755
☐	AD0107	£58.95	EALING Engines Design	Trevor Miles	01336-010107
☐	AD0113	£99.32	BARROWS Associates	Mandy Brown	01554-664422

Record: 1 of 4

Fig. 14.24 Illustrating the AND Criteria with Different Fields.

The OR Criteria with the Same Field: If you include multiple criteria in one field only, then Access assumes that you are searching for records that meet any one of the specified criteria. For example, the criteria <50 or >100 in the field Amount, shown in Fig. 14.25, list the required records, only if the No in the Paid? field is inserted in both rows.

Field:	Paid?	InvoiceID	Amount	Name	Contact
Table:	Invoices	Invoices	Invoices	Customers	Customers
Sort:		Ascending			
Show:	✓	✓	✓	✓	✓
Criteria:	No		<50		
or:	No		>100		

Paid?	Invoice ID	Amount	Name	Contact	Phone
☐	AD0102	£180.22	PARKWAY Gravel	James Stone	01534-987654
☐	AD0104	£111.56	GLOWORM Ltd	Peter Summers	01432-746523
☐	AD0106	£35.87	WORMGLAZE Ltd	Richard Glazer	01123-654321
☐	AD0108	£290.00	HIRE Service Equipment	Nicole Webb	01875-558822
☐	AD0109	£150.00	EUROBASE Co. Ltd	Sarah Star	01736-098765
☐	AD0111	£120.84	VORTEX Co. Ltd	Brian Storm	01776-223344
☐	AD0112	£135.00	AVON Construction	John Waters	01657-113355
☐	AD0114	£140.00	WESTWOOD Ltd	Mary Slim	01234-667755

Record: 1 of 8

Fig. 14.25 Illustrating the OR Criteria with the Same Field.

The OR Criteria with Different Fields: If you include multiple criteria in different fields, but in different rows, then Access assumes that you are searching for records that meet either one or the other of the specified criteria. For example, the criteria Yes in the Paid? field and the criteria <50 in the Amount field, but in different rows, list the following records.

Field:	Paid?		InvoiceID	Amount	Name	Contact
Table:	Invoices		Invoices	Invoices	Customers	Customers
Sort:			Ascending			
Show:		☑	☑	☑	☑	☑
Criteria:	Yes					
or:				<50		

	Paid?	Invoice ID	Amount	Name	Contact	Phone
▶	☑	AD0105	£123.45	SILVERSMITH Co	Adam Smith	01336-997755
	☐	AD0106	£35.87	WORMGLAZE Ltd	Richard Glazer	01123-654321
	☑	AD0110	£103.52	AVON Construction	John Waters	01657-113355
*	☐					

Record: 14 ◄ 1 ► ►I ►* of 3

Fig. 14.26 Illustrating The OR Criteria with Different Fields.

The AND and OR Criteria Together: The following choice of criteria will cause Access to retrieve either records that have Yes in the Paid? field and the company's name starts with the letter A, or records that the invoice amount is less than £50.

Field:	Paid?		InvoiceID	Amount	Name	Contact
Table:	Invoices		Invoices	Invoices	Customers	Customers
Sort:			Ascending			
Show:		☑	☑	☑	☑	☑
Criteria:	Yes				Like "A*"	
or:				<50		

	Paid?	Invoice ID	Amount	Name	Contact	Phone
▶	☐	AD0106	£35.87	WORMGLAZE Ltd	Richard Glazer	01123-654321
	☑	AD0110	£103.52	AVON Construction	John Waters	01657-113355
*	☐					

Record: 14 ◄ 1 ► ►I ►* of 2

Fig. 14.27 Illustrating the AND and OR Criteria Together.

Calculating Totals in Queries

Access allows you to perform calculations on groups of records. For example, we could find the total value of unpaid invoices grouped by month. To do this, start a new query in Design View, and using the Invoices table, drag the 'Paid?' And 'Amount' fields into the Query window, as shown below. Then enter in the third column (Field row) the formula

```
Month:DatePart("m",(Date))
```

Functions, such as 'sum', are entered in the Total row of a Σ query which can be displayed by clicking the **Totals** button, shown to the left, while in Design View. Save this query under the name 'Monthly Invoices', then click the **Run** button on the Toolbar to see the result.

Field:	Paid?	Amount	Month: DatePart("m",([Date]))
Table:	Invoices	Invoices	
Total:	Group By	Sum	Group By
Sort:			
Show:	☑	☑	☑
Criteria:	No		
or:			

Use the **File**, **Save As** menu command to save this query as 'Total Monthly Unpaid Invoices'.

Fig. 14.28. Calculating Totals in Queries.

* * *

We hope we have covered enough features of the program in this book to give you the foundations needed to make you want to explore Access more fully by yourself.

However, if you would prefer to be guided through these and additional topics, in much more detail, then may we suggest you keep a lookout for our forthcoming book *Microsoft Access 2003 explained*, also to be published by BERNARD BABANI (publishing) Ltd., if demand justifies.

15

Sharing Information

You can link or embed all or part of an existing file created either in an Office application or in any other application that supports Object Linking and Embedding (OLE). However, if an application does not support OLE, then you must use the copy/cut and paste commands to copy or move information from one application to another. In general, you copy, move, link, embed, or hyperlink information depending on the imposed situation, as follows:

Imposed Situation	Method to Adopt
Inserted information will not need updating, or Application does not support OLE.	Copy or move
Inserted information needs to be automatically updated in the destination file as changes are made to the data in the source file, or Source file will always be available and you want to minimise the size of the destination file, or Source file is to be shared amongst several users.	Link
Inserted information might need to be updated but source file might not be always accessible, or Destination file needs to be edited without having these changes reflected in the source file.	Embed
To jump to a location in a document or Web page, or to a file that was created in a different program.	Hyperlink

Copying or Moving Information

To copy or move information between programs running under Windows, such as Microsoft applications, is extremely easy. To move information, use the drag and drop facility, while to copy information, use the **Edit, Copy** and **Edit, Paste** commands.

To illustrate the technique, we will copy the **Project 3.xls** file, created in Excel, into Word. We will consider the following two possibilities:

Source File Available without Application

Let us assume that you only have the source file **Project 3.xls** on disc, but not the application that created it (that is you don't have Excel). In such a situation, you can only copy the contents of the whole file to the destination (in our case Word). To achieve this, do the following:

- Start Word and minimise it on the Taskbar.

- Use My Computer (or Explorer) to locate the file whose contents you want to copy into Word.

- Click the filename that you want to copy, hold the mouse button down and point to Word on the Taskbar until the application opens.

Fig. 15.1 Copying a Data File into an Application.

- While still holding the mouse button down, move the mouse pointer into Word's open document to the exact point where you would like to insert the contents of **Project 3.xls**.

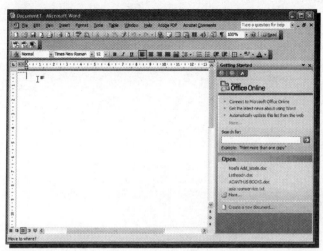

Fig. 15.2 Selecting the Point in an Application in which to Copy Data.

- Release the mouse button to place the contents of **Project 3.xls** into Word at that point.

Project Analysis: Adept Consultants Ltd.				
	Jan	Feb	Mar	1st Quarter
Income	£14,000.00	£15,000.00	£16,000.00	£45,000.00
Costs:				
Wages	£ 2,000.00	£ 3,000.00	£ 4,000.00	£ 9,000.00
Travel	£ 400.00	£ 500.00	£ 600.00	£ 1,500.00
Rent	£ 300.00	£ 300.00	£ 300.00	£ 900.00
Heat/Light	£ 150.00	£ 200.00	£ 130.00	£ 480.00
Phone/Fax	£ 250.00	£ 300.00	£ 350.00	£ 900.00
Adverts	£ 1,100.00	£ 1,200.00	£ 1,300.00	£ 3,600.00
Total Costs	£ 4,200.00	£ 5,500.00	£ 6,680.00	£ 16,380.00
Profit	£ 9,800.00	£ 9,500.00	£ 9,320.00	£ 28,620.00
Cumulative	£ 9,800.00	£ 19,300.00	£ 28,620.00	

Fig. 15.3 The Copied Data within an Application.

Source File and Application Available

Assuming that you have both the file and the application that
created it on your computer, you can copy all or part of the
contents of the source file to the destination file, as follows:

• Start Excel and open **Project 3.xls**, then highlight the
information to copy, change its format from **Currency**
to **Custom** so that the £ sign appears just in front of
the numbers and click the **Copy** button on the Toolbar.

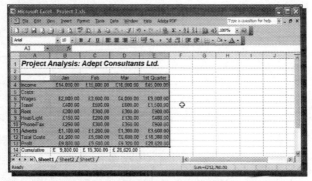

Fig. 15.4 Selecting Data to be Copied to Clipboard.

• Start Word and click the **Paste** button on the Toolbar.
Then select the first option from the Smart Tag list.

Fig. 15.5 Pasting Data into Application from the Clipboard.

Object Linking and Embedding

Object Linking is copying information from one file (the source file) to another file (the destination file) and maintaining a connection between the two files. When information in the source file is changed, then the information in the destination file is automatically updated. Linked data is stored in the source file, while the file into which you place the data stores only the location of the source and displays a representation of the linked data.

For example, you would use Object Linking if you would want an Excel chart included in, say, a Word document to be updated whenever you changed the information used to create the chart in the first place within Excel. In such a case, the Excel worksheet containing the chart would be referred to as the source file, while the Word document would be referred to as the destination file.

Object Embedding is inserting information created in one file (the source file) into another file (the container file). After such information has been embedded, the object becomes part of the container file. When you double-click an embedded object, it opens in the application in which it was created in the first place. You can then edit it in place, and the original object in the source application remains unchanged.

Thus, the main differences between linking and embedding are where the data is stored and how it is updated after you place it in your file. Linking saves you disc space as only one copy of the linked object is kept on disc. Embedding a logo chosen for your headed paper, saves the logo with every saved letter!

In what follows, we will discuss how you can link or embed either an entire file or selected information from an existing file, and how you can edit an embedded object. Furthermore, we will examine how to mail merge a letter written in Word with a list created either in Access, Excel, Outlook, or even Word itself.

Inserting a Picture

To insert a picture into an application, do the following:

- Open the container file, say Word, and click where you want to embed the new object.

- Use the **Insert, Picture** command, to display the additional drop-down menu, shown in Fig. 15.6.

As an example, we selected **Clip Art** (you could select **From File** to insert your own picture) and chose the picture shown in Fig. 15.7. Double-clicking the picture embeds it in Word.

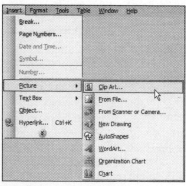

Right-clicking the picture displays a drop-down menu and selecting, first the **Show Picture Toolbar**, then the **Format Picture** options, places the Picture Toolbar on the screen and opens up the Format Picture dialogue box. Using these two

Fig. 15.6 Using the Insert Picture Menu.

options you can format and edit your picture to your requirements. Do try it for yourself.

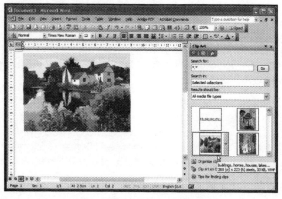

Fig. 15.7 Inserting a Picture.

Linking or Embedding an Entire File

To embed an existing file in its entirety into another application, do the following:

- Open the container file, say Word, and click where you want to embed the file.

- Use the **Insert, Object** command, to open the Object dialogue box, shown below, when the **Create from File** tab is clicked.

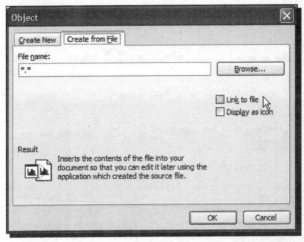

Fig. 15.8 Finding a File to Link or Embed into an Application.

To locate the file you want to link or embed, click **Browse**, and then select the options you want.

- In the **File name** box, type the name of the file you want to link or embed.

- To maintain a link to the original file, check the **Link to file** box.

If you want to insert a new application file, such as an Excel worksheet into Word, then use the **Create New** tab, scroll down the list of the displayed objects to the Microsoft Excel Worksheet, and click the **OK** button of the dialogue box. A new worksheet is inserted into the containing application.

Linking or Embedding Selected Information

To link or embed selected information from an existing file created in one application into another, do the following:

- Select the information in the source file you want to link or embed.

- Use the **Edit, Copy** command to copy the selected information to the Clipboard.

- Switch to the container file or document in which you want to place the information, and then click where you want the information to appear.

- Use the **Edit, Paste** command to paste the selected information into your document, then click the Smart Tag to display a list of options as shown in Fig. 15.9.

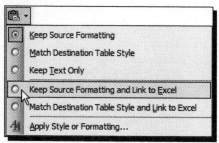

Fig. 15.9 The Smart Tag List of Paste Options.

- To link the information, click the **Keep Source Formatting and Link to Excel** option, or to embed the information, click the **Keep Source Formatting** option. As you can see, Word (the destination application) sensed that the information we were pasting came from Excel.

Copying information from another word processor, say Lotus Word Pro as in this case, shrinks the Smart Tag list of options as shown to the right, but with sufficient number to complete the job.

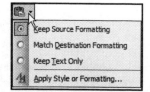

Hypertext Links

The main applications in Office 2003, Word, Excel, Access, PowerPoint, and Publisher, support hyperlinks. A hyperlink causes a jump to another location in the current document or Web page, to a different Word document or Web page, or to a file that was created in a different program. You can, for example, jump from a Word document to an Excel worksheet or to a PowerPoint slide to see more detail.

A hyperlink is represented by a 'hot' image or by display text (which is often blue and underlined) that you click to jump to a different location. To insert a hyperlink into any of the above mentioned Office 2003 application files or Web pages, select the display text or image, and either use the **Insert, Hyperlink** command or click the **Insert Hyperlink** button on the Standard Toolbar. Either action opens a dialogue box which allows you to browse for the destination address.

To illustrate the procedure, start Word, open the **PC User4** memo, and highlight the word 'Explorer' to be found towards the end of it. Next, click the **Hyperlink** button and locate the **explorer.exe** file (in the **Windows** folder), as shown below.

Fig. 15.10 Creating a Hyperlink in a Document.

Pressing the **OK** button, underlines the highlighted text and changes its colour to red. Pointing to such a hyperlink, while

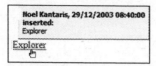

the <Ctrl> key is depressed, changes the mouse pointer to a hand, as shown here, and left-clicking it, starts the Explorer. When you have finished using the Explorer, click its **Close** button for the program to return you automatically to the hyperlinked Word document.

To remove a hyperlink, place the insertion pointer within the hyperlink word, click the **Insert Hyperlink** button again, and press the **Remove Link** button at the bottom right of the displayed Edit Hyperlink dialogue box.

As a second example, let us add to the **PC Users4** memo the following lines:

Hyperlinks can be used for displaying additional information, such as an Excel sheet, or a PowerPoint slide.

and save the result as **PC User5**. However, before you can use a range of cells in an Excel Workbook as your hyperlinked object, you must first name such a range. Therefore, start Excel, open the **Project 9** file and highlight the cell range A3:F13 in the Consolidation sheet, then use the **Insert, Name, Define** command and in the **Names in workbook** text box type Year_Summary (named ranges mustn't have spaces between words, hence the underscore). Next, save your changes to **Project 9** and exit Excel.

Fig. 15.11 Naming an Excel Range.

Finally, select the word 'sheet' in the Word document to use it as the hyperlink to **Project 9.xls** and browse to the location of the required file, then type after the filename the hash (#) character followed by the name of the required range, as shown below.

Fig. 15.12 Locating File and Named Range to be Hyperlinked into Word.

Left-clicking the hyperlink in Word will start Excel, open up the **Project 9** file, and display the named 'Year_Summary' range.

For the PowerPoint object, you could select the words 'PowerPoint slide' to use as the hyperlink to **Training 3.ppt**. If you wanted to make the link to a specific slide, then type # followed by the number of the required slide. Below we show the full address of such a hyperlink.

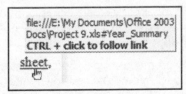

Fig. 15.13 The Address of a Hyperlink.

Using Mail Merge

There are times when you may want to send the same basic letter to several different people, or companies. The easiest way to do this is with a Mail Merge operation. Two files are prepared; a 'Data' file with the names and addresses, and a 'Form' file, containing the text and format of the letter. The two files are then merged together to produce a third file containing an individual letter to each party listed in the original data file.

Before creating a list of names and addresses for a mail merge, you need to select the Office application that is most suited to the task. For a mail merge, you can use a list you create in Access, Excel, Outlook, or Microsoft Word.

*   For a long list in which you expect to add, change, or delete records, and for which you want a powerful sorting and searching capability at your disposal, you should use either Access or Excel, then specify the appropriate data file in the Word Mail Merge.

*   To use the list of names and addresses in your Outlook Contact List, you select this list in the Word **Mail Merge** Task Pane.

*   For a small to medium size list of names and addresses in which you do not expect to make many changes, you could elect to create a list in the Word **Mail Merge** Task Pane.

We will illustrate the merge procedure by using a memo created in Word (**PC User1**) and a table which can be created in Word, or already exists either in an electronic book such as Outlook, in Excel or in an Access table such as Customers in **Adept 1**.

No matter which method you choose, first start Word and open the **PC User1** memo (or your own letter), then provide two empty lines at the very top of the memo/letter by placing the insertion pointer at the beginning of the memo and pressing <Enter> twice. Then select these two empty lines and choose the Normal paragraph style.

Next, select **Tools, Letters and Mailings, Mail Merge**, which displays the Mail Merge Task Pane shown in Fig. 15.14 below.

In this Task Pane, you define in six successive steps:

1. The document type to be used.

2. Whether to use the current document.

3. The source of your data - create a new list or use and existing one.

4. Write your letter if not already written, and select type of insert (such as Address block or Greeting line).

5. Preview your letters.

6. Complete merge by printing or editing individual letters.

Fig. 15.14 Mail Merge
Task Pane.

In what follows, we will examine each of these steps. You can, of course, skip the Create an Address List in Word section, if you already have an existing data list.

Creating an Address List in Word

On the third **Mail Merge** Task Pane option, click the **Type a new list** radio button, then click the **Create** link. In the displayed New Address List dialogue box, click the **Customize** button to display the Customize Address List dialogue box shown in Fig. 15.15.

Fig. 15.15 The Customize Address List Dialogue Box.

As you can see, Word provides commonly used field names for your address list. Unwanted field names can be deleted from the list by selecting them and pressing the **Delete** button. To add your own field name, click the **Add** button and supply details in the displayed dialogue box. The **Move** buttons can be used to move a selected field in the list up or down. Finally, an existing field name can be renamed by highlighting it then pressing the **Rename** button and supplying a different name.

Having compiled the required field names for your list, press the **OK** button to display the New Address List dialogue box, shown in Fig. 15.16 in which you can add the names of your contacts.

Fig. 15.16 Filling in the New Address List Dialogue Box.

Having completed your list, click the **Close** button which displays a Save Address List dialogue box, shown in Fig. 15.17, for you to name your data list, say **Customers**; Word adds the file extension **.mdb**.

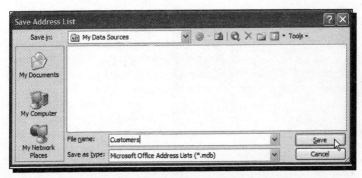

Fig. 15.17 The Save Address List Dialogue Box.

Getting an Address List

On the third **Mail Merge** Task Pane option, you can either use the newly created address list or you can select a different list. You can even edit a list by selecting it and clicking the **Edit** button which displays the Mail Merge Recipient dialogue box ready for you to edit, as shown in Fig. 15.18.

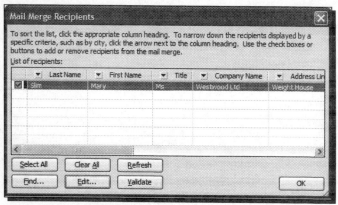

Fig. 15.18 The Mail Merge Recipients Dialogue Box.

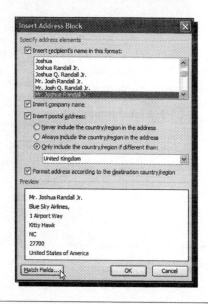

Having edited your list, first click the **OK** button, then the **Next** link at the bottom of the **Mail Merge** Task Pane to go to the fourth step in which you can click the **Address block** link to display the Insert Address Block box shown in Fig. 15.19. From here you can choose the way the recipient's address will display.

Fig. 15.19 The Insert Address Block Box.

If you have renamed fields or are using an external data file that does not contain the exact default fields displayed in Fig. 15.15, you will need to click the **Match Fields** button on the dialogue box in Fig. 15.19 to open the Match Fields dialogue box shown in Fig. 15.20 below.

Fig. 15.20 The Match Fields Dialogue Box.

Having matched the fields from your data to the default fields, click **OK** button on each opened dialogue box to obtain:

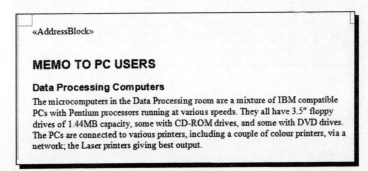

Selecting the entry <<<<AddressBlock>>>> at the top of the letter, then right-clicking displays a drop-down menu with options to **Edit Address Block** or **Toggle Field Codes**, to mention but a few. Selecting the latter option reveals the following:

Fig. 15.21 The Field Codes of the Address Block.

By studying these codes of the first four lines you will soon find out how to separate information differently, if you wish to. If you leave these codes as they are, going to the fifth step of the **Mail Merge** Task Pane displays the recipient's address at the top of your letter as shown in Fig. 15.22.

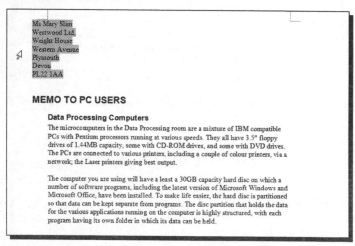

Fig. 15.22 The Preview of a Merged Letter.

The last step in the **Mail Merge** Task Pane allows you to print all your letters or edit individual letters. That's all there is to it. You will possibly find it takes as little time to do, as it did to read about it!

Appendix A

Office Screen Areas

The Microsoft Office 2003 applications screens are divided into several areas (not all applications have all the listed areas) which have the following functions:

Area	*Function*
Command buttons	Clicking on the command button, (see upper-left corner of the application window), displays a pull-down menu which can be used to control the program window. It allows you to restore, move, size, minimise, maximise, and close the window. Other Office applications have a different icon, as shown here for Word.
Title Bar	The bar at the top of a window which displays the application name and the name of the current document.
Minimise Button	When clicked on, this button minimises Word to an icon on the Windows Taskbar.
Restore Button	When clicked on, this button restores the active window to the position and size that was occupied before it was maximised.
	The restore button is then replaced by a Maximise button, as shown here, which is used to set the window to full screen size.

Close button   The extreme top right button that you click to close a window.

Menu Bar   The bar below the Title bar which allows you to choose from several menu options. Clicking on a menu item displays the pull-down menu associated with that item.

Type a Question Box   The text box at the far right of the menu bar. You can type in a help query and press the <Enter> key to get a listing of matching topics.

Standard Toolbar   The bar below the Menu bar which contains buttons that give you mouse click access to the functions most often used in the program.

Formatting Bar   The buttons on the Formatting Bar allow you to change the attributes of a font, such as italic and underline, and also to format text in various ways. The Formatting Bar contains three boxes; a style box, a font box and a size box to give instant access to all the installed styles, fonts and character sizes.

Rulers   The horizontal and vertical bars (where you can see and set page margins, tabulation points and indents.

Split Box   The area above the top vertical scroll button which when dragged allows you to split the screen.

Task Pane   The pane which presents help, formatting options and other relevant controls on the right-hand side of an application's screen.

Scroll Bars	The areas on the screen that contain scroll boxes in vertical and horizontal bars. Clicking on these bars allows you to control the part of a document which is visible on the screen.
Scroll Arrows	The arrowheads at each end of each scroll bar which you can click to scroll the screen up and down one line, or left and right 10% of the screen, at a time.
Insertion pointer	The pointer used to indicate where text will be inserted.
Views Buttons	Clicking these buttons changes screen views quickly.
Status Bar	The bottom line of a document's window that displays status information.

Appendix B

The Menu and Tasks Options

Menu Bar Options

Each menu bar option in a Microsoft Office application has associated with it a pull-down sub-menu. To activate a menu, either press the <Alt> key, which causes the first option of the menu (in this case the **File** menu option) to be selected, then use the right and left arrow keys to highlight any of the options in the menu, or use the mouse to point to an option. Pressing either the <Enter> key, or the left mouse button, reveals the pull-down sub-menu of the highlighted menu option. The sub-menu of the **File** option in Word is shown below.

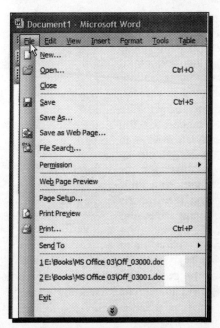

Fig. B.1 Word's File Sub Menu.

Note that as in the previous version of Office, the drop-down sub-menu displays only the most important options, but you have the option to view the full sub-menu by highlighting the double arrowheads at the bottom of it, by either pointing to that part of the sub-menu with the mouse or using the down-arrow cursor key to move the highlighted bar down.

The full sub-menu of the **File** menu option is displayed here in Fig. B.2 below. However, the order of your sub-menu options in both the short and the full version of the sub-menu could differ from ours. This is because Word learns from your actions and automatically promotes the items you choose from menu extensions on to the shortened version of the sub-menu.

Menu options can also be activated directly by pressing the <Alt> key followed by the underlined letter of the required option. Thus, pressing <Alt+F>, opens the pull-down **File** sub-menu. You can use the up and down arrow keys to move the highlighted bar up and down a sub-menu, or the right and left arrow keys to move along the options in the menu bar. Pressing the <Enter> key selects the highlighted option or

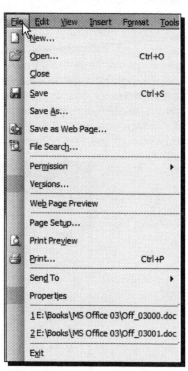

Fig. B.2 Word's Full File Sub Menu.

executes the highlighted command. Pressing the <Esc> key once, closes the pull-down sub-menu, while pressing the <Esc> key for a second time, closes the menu system.

Some of the sub-menu options can be accessed with 'quick key' combinations from the keyboard. Such combinations are shown on the drop-down menus, for example, <Ctrl+S> is the quick key for the **Save** option in the **File** sub-menu. If a sub-menu option is not available at any time, it will display in a grey colour. Some menu options only appear in Word when that tool is being used.

To get more details about any of the menu options, simply use the **Tools**, **Options** menu command. This opens the dialogue box shown here in Fig. B3.

Fig. B.3 Word's Options Dialogue Box.

Obviously the content of the various sub-menus and the Options dialogue box will be different for different Office 2003 application, but the principle of operation is the same.

Shortcut Menus

Context-sensitive shortcut menus are now one of Windows' most useful features. If you click the right mouse button on any screen feature, or document, a shortcut menu is displayed with the most frequently used commands relating to the type of work you were doing at the time. Most Microsoft Office applications have also combined 'smart tags' as part of the shortcut menu system. These automatically link related features or data to the situation involved.

The composite screen dump in Fig. B.4 below shows in turn the shortcut menus that open when selected text in Word, or the Toolbar area is right-clicked. In the first shortcut menu the **Cut** and **Copy** commands only become effective if you have text selected.

Fig. B.4 Example Shortcut Menus.

So, whatever you are doing in Office applications, you have rapid access to a menu of relevant functions by right-clicking your mouse. Left-clicking the mouse on an open menu selection will choose that function, while clicking on an area outside the shortcut menu (or pressing the <Esc> key), closes down the shortcut menu.

Task Panes

More of the common tasks in Office 2003 applications can now be carried out in Task Panes that display on the right side of an application's or document's window. For example, in Word you can quickly create new documents or open files using the Task Pane that appears when you first start the program. The **Search Results** Task pane gives you easy access to an application's file search facilities, or you can visually pick from a gallery of items in the Office **Clip Art** Task Pane.

Fig. B.5 The Task Pane List.

Fig. B.5 shows the **Getting Started** Task Pane with its control buttons partly obscured near the top. Once you select a Task Pane, the left and right arrows are totally visible (see Fig. B.4) and let you quickly move between the Task Panes you have open, while the down arrow (pointed to in Fig. B.5) opens the drop-down list of the available tasks, as shown here. The **x** button lets you close the pane. To reopen it you use the **View**, **Task Pane** menu command, or use the <Ctrl+F1> keys.

Glossary of Terms

Access control	A security mechanism that determines which operations a user is authorised to perform on a PC, a file, a printer, etc.
Active	Describes the folder, window or icon that you are currently using or that is currently selected.
Add-in	A mini-program which runs in conjunction with another and enhances its functionality.
Address	A unique number or name that identifies a specific computer or user on a network.
Administrator	For Windows XP Professional, a person responsible for setting up and managing local computers, their user and group accounts, and assigning passwords and permissions.
Applet	A program that can be downloaded over a network and launched on the user's computer.
Application	Software (program) designed to carry out certain activity, such as word processing, or data management.
Association	An identification of a filename extension to a program.
Attachment	A file that is added to an e-mail message for transmission.

Authoring	The process of creating web documents or software.
AVI	Audio Video Interleaved. A Windows multimedia file format for sound and moving pictures.
Background	An image, colour or texture which forms the background of a Web page or document.
Backup	To make a back-up copy of a file or a disc for safekeeping.
Baud rate	The speed at which a modem communicates.
Boot up	To start your computer by switching it on, which initiates a self test of its Random Access Memory (RAM), then loads the necessary system files.
Bound control	A control on a database form, report or data access page that is tied to a field in an underlying table or query.
Broadband	A communications systems in which the medium of transmission (such as a wire or fibre-optic cable) carries multiple messages at a time.
Browse	A button in some Windows dialogue boxes that lets you view a list of files and folders before you make a selection. Also to view a Web page.
Browser	A program, like the Internet Explorer, that lets you view Web pages.

Button	A graphic element or icon in a dialogue box or toolbar that performs a specified function.
Bytes	A unit of data that holds a single character, such as a letter, a digit.
Cable modem	A device that enables a broadband connection to the Internet by using cable television infrastructure.
CD-R	Recordable compact disc.
CD-ROM	Compact Disc - Read Only Memory; an optical disc which information may be read from but not written to.
CD-RW	Rewritable compact disc. Data can be copied to the CD on more than one occasion and can be erased.
Client	A computer that has access to services over a computer network. The computer providing the services is a server.
Clipboard	A temporary storage area of memory, where text and graphics are stored with the cut and copy actions. The Office clipboard can store up to 24 items.
Command	An instruction given to a computer to carry out a particular action.
Configuration	A general purpose term referring to the way you have your computer set up.
Context menu	A menu that opens when you right-click the mouse button on a feature.

Controls	Objects on a form, report, or data access page that display data, perform actions, or are used for decoration.
Cookies	Files stored on your hard drive by your Web browser that hold information for it to use.
Data access page	A Web page, created by Access, that has a connection to a database; you can view, add, edit, and manipulate the data in this page.
Database	A collection of data related to a particular topic or purpose.
DBMS	Database management system - A software interface between the database and the user.
Default	The command, device or option automatically chosen.
Desktop	The Windows screen working background.
Device driver	A special file that must be loaded into memory for Windows to be able to address a specific procedure or hardware device.
Device name	A logical name used by an operating system to identify a device, such as LPT1 or COM1 for the parallel or serial printer.
Dial-up Connection	A popular form of Net connection for the home user, over standard telephone lines.
Dialogue box	A window displayed on the screen to allow the user to enter information.

Digital signature

A means for originators of a message, file, or other digitally encoded information to bind their identity to the information.

Direct Connection

A permanent connection between your computer system and the Internet.

Directory

An area on disc where information relating to a group of files is kept. Also known as a folder.

Disc

A device on which you can store programs and data.

Disconnect

To detach a drive, port or computer from a shared device, or to break an Internet connection.

Document

A file produced by an application program. When used in reference to the Web, a document is any file containing text, media or hyperlinks that can be transferred from a server to a browser.

Domain

A group of devices, servers and computers on a network.

Domain Name

The name of an Internet site which allows you to reference Internet sites without knowing their true numerical address.

Double-click

To quickly press and release a mouse button twice.

Download

To transfer to your computer a file, or data, from another computer.

DPI	Dots Per Inch - a resolution standard for laser printers.
Drag	To move an object on the screen by pressing and holding down the left mouse button while moving the mouse.
Drive name	The letter followed by a colon which identifies a floppy or hard disc drive.
Drop-down list	A menu item that can be clicked to open extra items that can be selected.
E-mail	Electronic Mail - A system that allows computer users to send and receive messages electronically.
Embedded object	Information in a document that is 'copied' from its source application. Selecting the object opens the creating application from within the document.
Engine	Software used by search services.
File extension	The suffix following the period in a filename. Windows uses this to identify the source application program. For example **.mdb** indicates a Microsoft Access file.
Filename	The name given to a file. In Windows 95 and above this can be up to 256 characters long.
Filter	A set of criteria that is applied to data to show a subset of the data.

Firewall	Security measures designed to protect a networked system from unauthorised access.
Floppy disc	A removable disc on which information can be stored magnetically.
Folder	An area used to store a group of files, usually with a common link.
Font	A graphic design representing a set of characters, numbers and symbols.
Format	The structure of a file that defines the way it is stored and laid out on the screen or in print.
FTP	File Transfer Protocol. The procedure for connecting to a remote computer and transferring files.
Function key	One of the series of 10 or 12 keys marked with the letter F and a numeral, used for specific operations.
Gigabyte	(GB); 1,024 megabytes. Usually thought of as one billion bytes.
Graphic	A picture or illustration, also called an image. Formats include GIF, JPEG, BMP, PCX, and TIFF.
Hard copy	Output on paper.
Hard disc	A device built into the computer for holding programs and data.
Hardware	The equipment that makes up a computer system, excluding the programs or software.

Help
A Windows system that gives you instructions and additional information on using a program.

Home page
The document displayed when you first open your Web browser, or the first document you come to at a Web site.

Host
Computer connected directly to the Internet that provides services to other local and/or remote computers.

HTML
HyperText Markup Language, the format used in documents on the Web.

Hyperlink
A segment of text, or an image, that refers to another document on the Web, an Intranet or your PC.

Hypermedia
Hypertext extended to include linked multimedia.

Hypertext
A system that allows documents to be cross-linked so that the reader can explore related links, or documents, by clicking on a highlighted symbol.

Icon
A small graphic image, or button, that represents a function or object. Clicking on an icon produces an action.

Image
See graphic.

Insertion point
A flashing bar that shows where typed text will be entered into a document.

Interface	A device that allows you to connect a computer to its peripherals.
Internet	The global system of computer networks.
Intranet	A private network inside an organisation using the same kind of software as the Internet.
IP	Internet Protocol - The rules that provide basic Internet functions.
IP Address	Internet Protocol Address - every computer on the Internet has a unique identifying number.
ISP	Internet Service Provider - A company that offers access to the Internet.
JPEG/JPG	Joint Photographic Experts Group, a popular cross-platform format for image files - best suited for true colour original images.
Kilobyte	(KB); 1024 bytes of information or storage space.
LAN	Local Area Network - High-speed, privately-owned network covering an office or a building.
Linked object	An object that is inserted into a document but still exists in the source file. Changing the original object automatically updates it within the linked document.
Links	The hypertext connections between Web pages.
Location	An Internet address.
Log on	To gain access to a network.

Megabyte	(MB); 1024 kilobytes of information or storage space.
Megahertz	(MHz); Speed of processor in millions of cycles per second.
Memory	Part of computer consisting of storage elements organised into addressable locations that can hold data and instructions.
Menu	A list of available options in an application.
Menu bar	The horizontal bar that lists the names of menus.
Modem	Short for Modulator-demodulator devices. An electronic device that lets computers communicate electronically.
Monitor	The display device connected to your PC, also called a screen.
Mouse	A device used to manipulate a pointer around your display and activate processes by pressing buttons.
Multimedia	The use of photographs, music and sound and movie images in a presentation.
My Documents	A folder that provides a convenient place to store documents, graphics, or other files you want to access quickly.
Network	Two or more computers connected together to share resources.
Network server	Central computer which stores files for several linked computers.

OLE	Object Linking and Embedding - A technology for transferring and sharing information among software applications.
Online	Having access to the Internet.
Online Service	Services such as America On-line and CompuServe that provide content to subscribers and usually connections to the Internet.
Page	An HTML document, or Web site.
Parallel port	The input/output connector for a parallel interface device. Printers are generally plugged into a parallel port.
Partition	A portion of a physical disc that functions as though it were a physically separate disc.
Password	A unique character string used to gain access to a network, program, or mailbox.
Peripheral	Any device attached to a PC.
Pixel	A picture element on screen; the smallest element that can be independently assigned colour and intensity.
Plug-and-play	Hardware which can be plugged into a PC and be used immediately without configuration.
POP3	Post Office Protocol - a method of storing and returning e-mail.
Port	The place where information goes into or out of a computer, e.g. a modem might be connected to the serial port.

Print queue	A list of print jobs waiting to be sent to a printer.
Program	A set of instructions which cause a computer to perform tasks.
Query	The set of keywords and operators sent by a user to a search engine, or a database search request.
Queue	A list of e-mail messages waiting to be sent over the Internet.
RAM	Random Access Memory. The computer's volatile memory. Data held in it is lost when power is switched off.
Registered file type	File types that are tracked by the system registry and are recognised by the programs you have installed on your computer.
ROM	Read Only Memory. A PC's non-volatile memory. Data is written into this memory at manufacture and is not affected by power loss.
Scroll bar	A bar that appears at the right side or bottom edge of a window.
Search engine	A program that helps users find information across the Internet.
Server	A computer system that manages and delivers information for client computers.
Shortcut	A link to any item accessible on your computer or on a network, such as a program, file, folder, disc drive, Web page, printer, or another computer.

Site	A place on the Internet. Every Web page has a location where it resides which is called its site.
Smart tag	A button that when clicked, opens a shortcut menu to give fast access to other features or Office applications.
SMTP	Simple Mail Transfer Protocol - a protocol dictating how e-mail messages are exchanged over the Internet.
Software	The programs and instructions that control your PC.
Spamming	Sending the same message to a large number of mailing lists or newsgroups. Also to overload a Web page with excessive keywords in an attempt to get a better search ranking.
Spooler	Software which handles transfer of information to a store to be used by a peripheral device.
SQL	Structured Query Language, used with relational databases.
Surfing	The process of looking around the Internet.
SVGA	Super Video Graphics Array; it has 256, or more, colours.
Task Pane	A pane or sub-window that gives a range of options pertaining to the task currently being performed.
Text file	An unformatted file of text characters saved in ASCII format.

Thumbnail	A small graphic image.
Toggle	To turn an action on and off with the same switch.
Toolbar	A bar containing buttons or icons giving quick access to commands.
TrueType fonts	Fonts that can be scaled to any size and print as they show on the screen.
URL	Uniform Resource Locator, the addressing system used on the Web, containing information about the method of access, the server to be accessed and the path of the file to be accessed.
User ID	The unique identifier, usually used in conjunction with a password, which identifies you on a computer.
Web	A network of hypertext-based multimedia information servers. Browsers are used to view any information on the Web.
Web Page	An HTML document that is accessible on the Web.
Wizard	A Microsoft tool that shows how to perform certain operations, or asks you questions and then creates an object depending on your answers.

Index

Companion Discs

COMPANION DISCS are available for most computer books written by the same author(s) and published by BERNARD BABANI (publishing) LTD, as listed at the front of this book (except for those marked with an asterisk). These books contain many pages of file/program listings. There is no reason why you should spend hours typing them into your computer, unless you wish to do so, or need the practice.

ORDERING INSTRUCTIONS

To obtain companion discs, fill in the order form below, or a copy of it, enclose a cheque (payable to **P.R.M. Oliver**) or a postal order, and send it to the address given below. **Make sure you fill in your name and address** and specify the book number and title in your order.

Book No.	Book Name	Unit Price	Total Price
BP		£3.50	
BP		£3.50	
BP		£3.50	
Name .... Address		Sub-total	£.............
		P & P (@ 45p/disc)	£.............
		Total Due	£.............
Send to: P.R.M. Oliver, West Trevarth House, West Trevarth, Nr Redruth, Cornwall, TR16 5TJ			

PLEASE NOTE

The author(s) are fully responsible for providing this Companion Disc service. The publishers of this book accept no responsibility for the supply, quality, or magnetic contents of the disc, or in respect of any damage, or injury that might be suffered or caused by its use.